A Humanitarian Essay Embodying Poetry

2천 권을 읽으면 알게 되는 것들

THINGS YOU KNOW WHEN YOU READ 2,000 BOOKS

MOONLIGHT LIBRARY

ELLA YOON

Published 2024 by Your Book Angel

Printed in the United States
Edited by Keidi Keating
Layout by Rochelle Mensidor

ISBN: 979-8-9897121-5-1

Table of Contents

ACKNOWLEDGEMENTS

Dreaming of a world accompanied by books,
I dedicate this book to the happiness of all humanity.

THE KEY TO HUMAN HAPPINESS: THE GLOBAL CULTURE OF 30-MINUTE MORNING READING

Thanks to Kyobo Bookstore, a franchise I stumbled upon by chance, I learned about the world of books. I could fully resonate with the slogan: "Books shape people, and people shape books," and I owe them my gratitude.

Reading books brought me so much joy, I've engaged with them every day for twenty years. I've experienced the full spectrum of emotions, from delight to sorrow, alongside books. Books have been with me before and after getting married, and even after my children were born. When it's rained, I've held my books close to my heart, scared they would get wet. From the time my child was in my womb to when she was born, books accompanied us. I would place my children's books alongside mine in the stroller and read them aloud when they were awake and read my own book when they fell asleep. I lay on the bench and read, gazing at the sky.

My heart filled with elation the day I encountered books for the first time, and from then forward, a new book always sparked my excitement and intrigue. The world of books is another realm within Earth.

For me, the essence of books always boiled down to happiness. They provide joy and offer opportunities to learn how to transform our lives into even happier experiences.

Twenty-odd years have passed since my introduction to books, and I can now answer the question, "What makes a life happy?" The secret to happiness lies in the small objects we are looking at right now. Within the pages of a book, there are adventures, love, gratitude, pleasure, and precious friendships, all of which impact our mental and emotional health. The more I drink clean water, the clearer my body becomes, and the more I drink pure water, the more aware I become of the impurities of my body. Similarly, the clarity and impurity of my mind can be discerned through books, and it is through the knowledge and experiences books provide that we can purify our minds.

But how can we bring this precious elixir of happiness closer to us? How can we drink it more often?

The Global Culture of 30-Minute Morning Reading

Reading is not just a personal hobby.
Its value extends far beyond the individual.

Have you not read
and experienced it yourself?

Is it truly impossible to devote 30 minutes
to reading each morning?

What if we shared books
with employees as gifts?

Work is not about the quantity of time spent,
but rather the quality of it.

Aren't books like a treasure island
to discover and explore?

A happy corporate culture is one
where the management embraces reading.

A happy environment in schools is one
that encourages education through reading.

I dream of a world that becomes happier with books.

Up until now, my reading was not about accumulating knowledge or wisdom. It was a dialogue with myself, mediated by the authors of those books. Perhaps I read within a bubble. Little did I know that 'real books' could be found outside of the physical pages.

A real book is everything in this world: nature, the universe, and humans—everything we see and experience that can impact our thoughts, behaviors, and decisions, everything that carried potential to be told to others through the spoken or written word. Each and every creation in this world is a 'book' of its own. Everything we see and everything we perceive is, in a sense, a letter or a story.

After many years of reading, I've finally came to understand the wise words of our ancestors who've read thousands of books, that stories are our companions.

It has taken two years to write this book. During this time, the Korea Institute of Human Resources Development in Science and Technology (KIRD) became a ray of hope, and I offer my thanks to the great masters who accepted the interview, adding immense value to these pages. I have poured the fruits of my reading over the years into this book in the hope that we can grow to cherish and love one another in harmony through purifying our minds. This book serves as a beautiful gift, birthed through the impressions of two thousand other books, to creating a happier nation and a happier humanity.

I dream of a rainbow-like Earth, united by books. **The key to a happier Earth lies within books. The practical approach is to establish a global culture of 30-minute morning reading at all workplaces and in schools. Books never betray our efforts. They reward us with the most honest results, albeit at different times.** May this small but precious book among the many bloom colorful flowers that can enrich our lives.

While the fragrance of each story's flower is unique, their letters lead us to a happier life. May we embrace this book as a bouquet of joy and fulfillment.

With heartfelt blessings, tinted with the magical hues of a beautiful sunset,

˜Ella Yoon

I RELISHED -
THE MOST FASCINATING THING IN THE WORLD: BOOKS

The most magical object in the world is a book

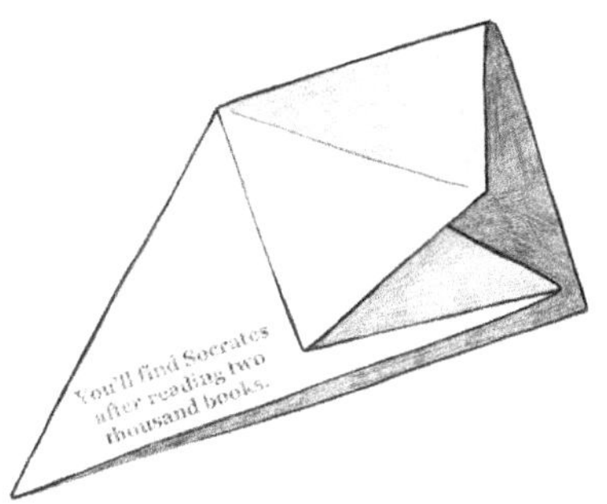

You'll Find Socrates After Reading Two Thousand Books

First Encounter with Books at the Gwanghwamun Kyobo Book Center

After graduating from university, my first workplace was located near Gwanghwamun Station. I had to walk past the Kyobo Book Center to get to the station after work. One day, I decided to head toward the bookstore instead of going straight home. The people browsing the shelves looked relaxed. Even the music that filled the space was perfect.

Ever since that day, the Kyobo Book Center became my personal haven. I stopped by the store every day after work. The books were neatly organized by categories. My heart skipped when I held a book I'd picked close to me. It felt as if I'd discovered a precious stone.

I read during my subway rides and waiting times, before going to bed, and even in the bathroom. To get home, I had to walk for twenty minutes after getting off the subway. I didn't want to waste a single minute, so I opened a book and read as I took steps slowly. Several times, I became so immersed in the pages, I almost collided with telephone poles. When it got dark, I would use the flashlight on my phone to continue reading my latest adventure.

As I came to savor the joy of reading, I set a goal.

To read 100 books in a year.

Books are another realm within Earth [Image source: Pixabay]

Reading a hundred books in a year while working meant I had to dedicate most of my time outside of work to reading.

I always carried two books and a pen in my bag. There were nights when I stayed up late reading, and on weekends, I often visited the library.

What Did I Learn After Reading 2,000 Books?

I gradually became deeply engrossed by the taste of reading. It was delightful to discover a diverse array of flavors, where the hearts of authors and my heart intersected.

After achieving my goal of reading a hundred books in the first year, it became natural to continue the practice the following year. The initial hurdle is always the most challenging. From 100 books to 200, then to 500, and as the years passed, I reached around 2,000 volumes. Stopping myself from reading became more difficult than continuing to read.

Following over ten years reading, I pondered why I limited myself to just consuming. I even questioned whether I had achieved anything and thought I might be nothing but a fool who only read books instead of giving back in honor of what I have received. So, I started writing. Rather, it would be more appropriate to say things poured out of me and onto the pages. It was as if something overflowed, just like water spilling over the brim of a cup

Then I encountered a sentence.

You'll find Socrates after reading two thousand books [Image source: Pixabay]

Know thyself. — Socrates

After reading every day for twenty years, I finally understood. Over 2,000 volumes boiled down to this single statement.

The water inside the cup was not knowledge, nor was it wisdom. It was nothing but becoming aware of my own inadequacies. That water was the product of my recognition of personal shortcomings and it led me back to learning. Learning about nature, objects, and people; learning connected to gratitude. Gratitude that was composed of cells of love.

In the end, I had studied the art of love.

Through these studies, I realized more than my personal shortcomings. I came to understand that humans don't truly teach one another. If anything teaches us, it's nature, which combines those lessons with enlightenment, offering us something deeper and more impactful than mere 'teachings.'

Life is about sharing the world we see within the confines of this planet called Earth. In the act of sharing, there is no right or wrong. There is no reason for us to fight as, at the end of the day, we're all flowers in the same field no matter how intelligent or inadequate one is. Flowers do not quarrel. They do not experience inferiority. They merely blossom and exist among one another in harmony.

Take a close look at the flowers along the roadside. Even in the harshest environments, they fulfill their roles. Whether big or small, they all eventually blossom and offer their pollen and beauty to the other creatures of the world. That is the order of nature. And aren't we also a part of nature?

Nature teaches us, and we in turn share with one another.

Water eventually meets the sea [Image source: Pixabay]

Do you find life challenging? Is the journey to your dreams arduous?

Let us seek wisdom from water. Water tenderly embraces even the sharpest corners. Water chooses to find a small crevice to pass around rocks in its path instead of climbing over it. Water doesn't break through the ice on a cold day. Rather, it waits for the ice to give way. It pierces through small openings and advances towards larger pools. Water has a clear destination—the sea, and it travels the path it must follow in silence. Water sustains life. It is power and can be overwhelming when treated as a combatant, but it always settles and returns to a flow state of peace and tranquility.

Similarly, books always welcome us. They long to meet us and take us away on journeys of knowledge and adventure. They don't mind whether it's dawn or dusk. If you're lonely on your own path, try taking a step closer to the open embrace of books and sharing the joy of reading. Like water quenches your thirst, satisfy the needs of your mind.

The best day to read books is today. The best time to read books is now.

The True Sages in Books Are Children

Raising my children, I realized they are the true sages in the pages and in the real book of life are, in fact, children. The wise beings I encountered were also children in a sense—adults who possess the innocence of a child's pure heart.

I came to understand the words of Mencius:

"The great person is someone who does not lose the heart of a child."

The key to happiness is learning the heart of a child [Image source: Pixabay]

Why do children possess such innocence? We are all born with beautiful hearts. However, as we live, our hearts undergo changes from the influences of the people and experiences around us. Children's hearts are complete, and a complete heart sees the world through the eyes of that heart. While adult hearts are scarred and potentially cracked and worn, those results aren't anyone's fault; they are just traces of life. And they are the aspects of ourselves that we should embrace tenderly.

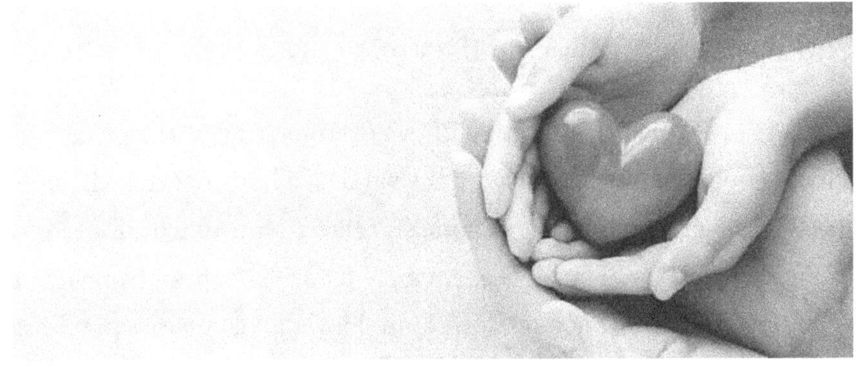

The love of a complete heart is like the sun [Image source: Pixabay]

The hearts of sages resemble those of children because they used the innocence of a child's heart to polish their own rough hearts.

As we come to understand the hearts of children, we also understand the hearts of sages. And as we understand the hearts of sages, we begin to understand ourselves and we can explore, embrace, and work with our shortcomings to transform.

Our lives are a journey of constant learning and growth.

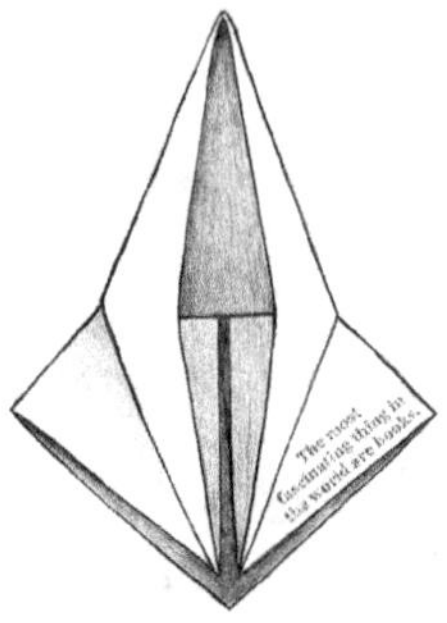

The Most Fascinating Thing
in the World Are Books

The most magical object in the world is a book

There is only one thing I buy without even looking at the price tag. That's a book. How much should the value of a book be? It is difficult to say. How much value should one star have? How much should the moon be valued at? The biggest reason why prices cannot be reached is because they contain a person's soul. How can a person's precious value be expressed in money? Books are like this, too. It is like the stars floating in the sky, like the gentle sun, and the peaceful moon.

Just enjoy the book

I sometimes get questions from readers who say they don't remember anything after reading a book. Do I need to remember the contents of the book? Books are like food. Do you need to remember what side dish you ate for breakfast? Just eat it deliciously. And all we need is a grateful heart. I hope you feel free from the burden of having to remember the contents of the book. Rather than remembering the ingredients in a book, you just need to remember how the book tastes. It's like when you eat a dish, you feel the rich flavor and atmosphere rather than considering the ingredients in the food. Don't the taste and atmosphere make us come back again? The same goes for books. If you like the taste and atmosphere, you'll come back again. The habit of reading comes first from knowing how to enjoy books. Once you know how to enjoy books, habits become natural.

When reading a book, you should always give yourself freedom. If you force yourself to read a book a day for a few minutes a day, your body will suffer. The purpose of reading is to free the soul. When our body is free, it can demonstrate its abilities.

There is no correct answer to the reading method

Is there a right answer to the reading method? Reading time is when our souls need to be most free. If I keep telling myself what to do at a time when my soul should be most free, it blocks my freedom. I just have to let my body do what it wants. As you read, your reading skills evolve. That development may not necessarily be an addition, but rather a subtraction. I hope you can take a step outside the framework set by someone else. The act of reading is a truly mystical activity in a beautiful place in our soul, reserved only for ourselves.

My reading method is thorough reading. I also underline and take notes in the book. For me, a pen is an indispensable and important tool. If I don't have a pen, I try not to read if possible. Because you can't walk through the next forest without underlining something. So books and pens are always like a pair for me. I hold on to it with an underline in case it runs away. The empty margins of the book are space for notes. This is where I get my thoughts out. Sometimes I write down ideas, and my resolutions, and sometimes I put a message of love for my child. If I have a different opinion or question from the author, I write down my thoughts. If I like a sentence, I write it down in the book. I even read aloud. Emoticons are sometimes used to express laughter or sadness. If a character I'm curious about appears in the book, I make a note saying, "I will look for more," and if I like a quoted sentence, I write, "I will read this book." If I like an author's books, I buy all of that author's books. So, when you read one book, you don't end up with just one book, but a list of books to read. A book calls out to another book.

To read is to let my soul smile [Image source: Pixabay]

I especially love those from the olden days. How can I express the broad and profound taste of old writings? I'm deeply grateful I can encounter them through books.

Let's explore the reading methods of three individuals interviewed by the Korea Institute of Human Resources Development in Science and Technology (KIRD) K-CLUB.

Professor Kim Beomjun, professor of Physics at Sungkyunkwan University
"I resolve to finish the book I chose to read no matter what, whether I like it or not."

Professor Yoo Yeongman, knowledge ecologist at Hanyang University
"I don't differentiate between reading and writing. Sometimes I write a book while reading, and sometimes I read a book while I write."

Professor Hwang Nongmun, materials engineering professor at Seoul National University
"I choose my books carefully, and once I choose, I read them several times. I underline important parts and jot down my thoughts along with what I need to remember. I mark questions with question marks.

"I rarely borrow books from the library because I need notes like this."

Our reading style is this different. However, one thing I would like to ask you is that although the reading method is a matter of personal preference, I hope that you read as thoroughly as possible. The three professors were also reading it thoroughly. The same goes for me too. If you don't read it carefully, you won't feel like you've eaten it. In my case, I can't taste the food. It feels like I'm only smelling the food without chewing it. I recommend reading it as thoroughly as possible. It is recommended that you chew your food thoroughly even if you eat a small amount rather than a large amount. The number of books is not important. As we eat, it naturally accumulates, and there is no need to count the number of foods we have eaten. Maybe it's like counting the number of bowls of rice I've eaten from.

The most important thing after reading a book is 'life application.' How should I apply what I ate to my life? What shall I bring into my life? Keywords picked from books are good, keywords picked by oneself are good, and it is about directly reflecting them in my organization and my life. How about 'one book and one practice'? The power of books is that small changes in habits reflected in my life come together to create a giant. You must believe in the power of books.

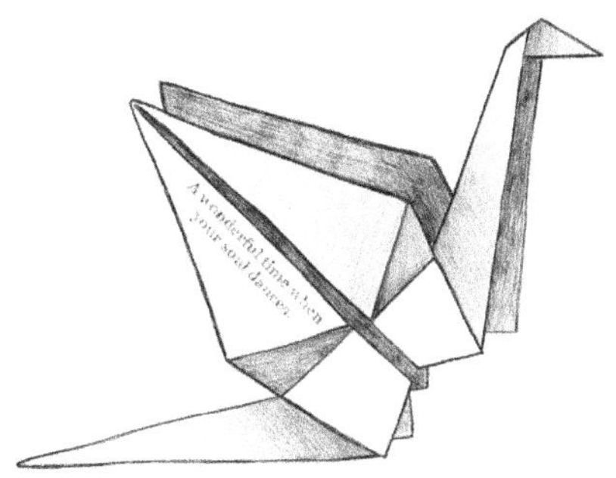

Reading A Book:
A Wonderful Time When
Your Soul Dances

The Pleasure of Being with the Best Companion

At the first encounter, there was excitement.
At the second encounter, I wanted to stay longer.
At the third encounter, I wanted us to be together.

My heart spoke, and my soul recognized
my lifelong, best companion.

We have always been together,
and we remain together today.

In the future, forever,
we will be together.

My great companion—
book companion.

Do you have a beautiful companion? Do you have a companion who understands your heart? The companionship of books knows when to speak and when to remain silent. A book always places us as the master. It always sets itself as the guest. The only master of our lives is ourselves, and although books can inform and guide and transform our experiences, we remain in control of their support. Who else can claim that role?

The book companion knows how to wait. It never rushes. It makes it easy to take a break to rest or tend to responsibilities or to spend time with other book companions. It invites us to come again whenever we want. It radiates an atmosphere of warmth, comfort, and tranquility. Whether we stay for a short while or a long time, it patiently waits. A book companion soothes our minds. If knowledge is needed, it provides; if wisdom is needed, it provides. If a change of mood is required, a book companion can help shift our mood.

Among the countless beauties of books, the greatest is the freedom it bestows upon our mind and soul.

A book companion always blurs the boundaries between reality and ideals. It sets no fences, allowing for vast and open exploration. It's a perfect place for your soul to leap and frolic. It presents freedom to our souls as a child would play on an expansive field. It allows for walking, running, and even lying down. The book companion knows that the boundaries between reality and ideals are merely walls created by thoughts, illusions fabricated solely by ourselves.

The Reason for the Joy of Befriending Books

Your forest of letters is always tranquil.
When my heart wavers, you hold me.
How delightful it is.

The gates of your forest are always open.
Like the sunlight shining evenly on all things,
you do not discriminate against any guests.

In your forest of letters, the songs of birds fill the air.
In your forest of letters, the murmuring of water flows.

Eyes brighten, ears soften.
In your company, I do not long for utopia.

Above all, the book companion is positive. It plants positivity, hence the sprouts of positivity grow. The power of positivity is immense. It possesses the skill to turn withering leaves into vibrant ones. The book companion is also a great listener. It shows courtesy when it speaks or listens.

The book companion draws out even the deepest thoughts. It gently encourages with a soft smile. It reassures us that it's alright, that things will get better. It suggests following the deeper inner voice, the voice of our true selves.

No wonder I find its company so pleasing as it reads my mind. Inner thoughts need no adornment; having one's authentic heart is sufficient.

The greatest beauty of a book companion is its ability to guide us to finding answers on our own. Although books express thoughts, they leave the conclusions up to us and allows us to take action for ourselves. The book companion merely welcomes you with open arms, no matter what you walk away with. Even the greatest book's true power of shaping ourselves lies in us taking action. The book companion can lead us to the edge of the vast ocean, but it's ourselves who must leap in and swim.

As You Develop a Taste for Books, Even the Characters Become Endearing

When you grow fond of books, you will grow fond of the words within them, and when you grow fond of the words, you will grow fond of the forest of letters. As you stroll through the forest of letters, they begin to dance and seep into you.

As I walk through the forest of dancing words, the beautiful text reminds me of King Sejong.

The Remarkable Magic of the Korean Alphabet, Hangul

As I delve deeper into the taste of books, their fragrance becomes even more delightful. The rustle of pages turning is also pleasing to the ears. The clean white space of the margins is truly wonderful too. The pause created by these spaces, leaving some squares in the forest of letters untouched, is equally pleasant. There is an order and rhythm to each element of each page.

As I read the words, the way consonants and vowels come together to form characters astonishes and amazes me. Characters—the script in which we form words in our various languages—have rules and order. It is truly a wondrous thing to have beautiful characters, and I often feel gratitude for the predecessors of our languages.

Hangul, the Korean alphabet, was created by King Sejong at the age of forty-six. According to the data introduced on the National Archives of Korea's official website, Hangul is the only script in the world whose creator, the date of proclamation, and the principles of the language are all known. The day Hangul was first created was in December of the lunar calendar in 1443 (the twenty-fifth year of King Sejong's reign). It was proclaimed to the whole nation three years later in September of the lunar calendar in 1446.

The name at that time is the well-known 'Hunminjeongeum,' which means 'the proper sounds for the instruction of the people'. Could there be a more fitting expression? The beautiful heart of King Sejong, who deeply loved his nation and its people, is wholly encapsulated in this word.

In 1927, the Korean Language Research Society, established in 1908 by Ju Si-gyeong (one of the founders of modern Korean linguistics) published *Hangul*, a journal, which led to its widespread use. The term Hangul has the meaning of 'great writing,' 'foremost writing,' or the 'one and only writing'. Let's take a moment to attend to the words of Ju Si-gyeong, known as the 'Father of Korean Orthography'.

"The growth of a tree is the work of the sky, while tending to that tree is the work of humans. What we must do is refine our language to speak and write it correctly."

*Source: Korean Wikipedia (주시경) — https://ko.wikipedia.org/wiki/주시경

The 4th King of Joseon Dynasty (King Sejong) - Gwanghwamun Square, Republic of Korea [Image source: Pixabay]

The principles of the creation of Hangul are intricately detailed in *Hunminjeongeum Haeryebon*, which King Sejong personally wrote and published through the scholars of Jiphyeonjeon (also known as The Hall of Worthies, a royal research institute). The book was designated as National Treasure No. 70 in October 1997 and was subsequently registered as a UNESCO Memory of the World. Though above all, the greatest beauty of Hangul lies in its simplicity. Among OECD countries, South Korea has the lowest illiteracy rate at 0.1%, primarily due to the ease with which anyone can learn Hangul.

Hangul is simple to read, smooth to listen to, and easy to write. From young children to adults, it's a script that all citizens can easily access. I recommend learning Hangul to those who want to learn a new language.

According to Wikipedia, the principle of the Hangul characters is based on "phonemic orthography," which involves observing the shape of the vocal organs when pronouncing a character. For instance, 'ㅁ' resembles the shape of lips, 'ㅇ' is similar to the shape of the throat, 'ㅅ' represents teeth, 'ㄱ' is like the tip of the tongue blocking the throat, and 'ㄴ' depicts the tongue touching the upper gums.

Watching young children easily learn Hangul, I was once again amazed by its excellence.

Hangul is so effective, it has even been officially adopted as the script for some indigenous groups around the world who previously had no writing system. I couldn't be prouder. I hope more people will consider learning Hangul as a second or third additional language.

Every language has its own spirit and love. Understanding a new language opens up a new world. Learning a language is akin to embracing the culture and love of that country. I dream of a world where the beautiful languages of the world dance together, united through encounters with books. Understanding characters—scripts—is where love begins.

Oral Recitation Imprints Characters on the Body

Thanks to King Sejong and the scholars of Jiphyeonjeon, we get to experience the richness of characters. Hangul is beautiful from all angles. It's upright and balanced. Above all, a book read in Hangul is always delightful. In ancient times, people believed that if you read a book out loud, the clear energy of the pronunciation would permeate one's body.

It's understandable how stories of scholars from the past reciting books, their clear voices ringing over walls, could flutter the hearts of maidens.

When did it all begin? After reading for a long time, recitation became a part of the experience. It happens naturally, not by intention. When I find a sentence worthy of focus, I find myself reciting it in addition to underlining it, a process which has reshaped the necessity of my retention method.

One day on the subway ride home, I needed to underline something, but I didn't have a pen on me—a grave error, to be missing a vital tool for my process. I asked the person next to me if he had a pen so I could use his pen to underline the book. The sentences I wanted to underline seemingly disappeared over time, fading back into the mass of other words.

At the time, I had to underline a sentence right at that moment to continue the journey through the subsequent text. But now, I can read without a pen, if necessary, thanks to recitation. After reciting the passage once, it's imprinted on my mind; twice, and it's imprinted stronger.

The more you repeat the same sentence, the deeper etched it becomes.

These inscribed sentences become my soul and the universe for my heart. However, recitation alone is not quite enough, it's merely a temporary hold until I can return to the passage with my trusty pen.

The more I savor, the essence of the characters—like the juice of a dish—oozes out. When I read borrowed books that I can't underline, I transcribe the text into a separate notebook. I press down hard as I write. The more meticulously I write each letter, the richer the taste and flavor of the meal becomes.

Chapter 2

I LEARNED – ALL THINGS WE SEE ARE BOOKS

The mirror called a book reflects all things

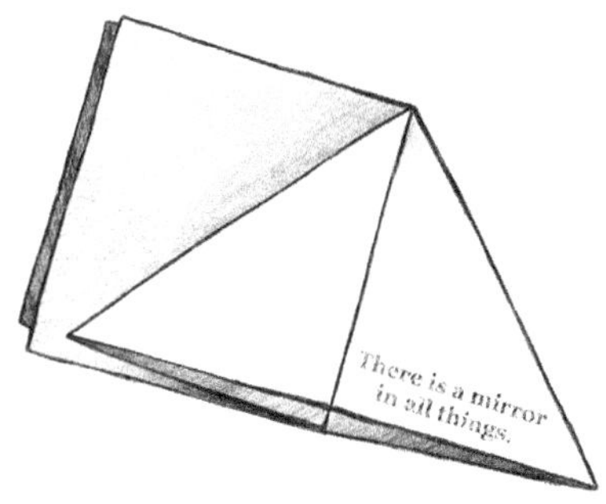

There Is a Mirror in All Things

All things in the world have mirrors. The sea is mirrored by the sky. The moon is mirrored by the sun. What about humans? Our mirror lies within our eyes. I found myself within the pupils of other people. When I smile, their eyes smile too. When I frown, their eyes also furrow. I am other people, and other people are me. The mirror that allows us all to see ourselves best is the mirror of humanity. It's through of the mirror within the pupils of others that we can introspect.

When the sky turns red, the sea also turns red [Image source: Pixabay]

To see the mirror, we must encounter another human being. But there are physical limitations to meeting countless people. We must coordinate meeting times, and physical distance and temporal constraints naturally apply. However, there is one thing that compensates for all of these: books.

Books are an extension of humanity. Reading a book is, in essence, meeting a person. In a single day, you can encounter several people or a single person in depth through books. Since books involve the meeting of souls, you can meet individuals from centuries past. There's no need to fret about different nationalities and unfamiliar languages. There are translators who are kind enough to convert the text for us.

Reading books is encountering people to look into the mirror. The more often you engage, the more closely you can scrutinize yourself. Just as the ocean sees the mirror of the sky, we can see ourselves through the mirror of books.

Reading: Into the Deep Sea

The time I delved the deepest into the sea of books was after getting married when I attended English language classes in Gangnam on weekends.

As the new year rolled in, the unchanging goal of my studies was English. It felt like I was running in place. When the time to study English approached in the middle of reading books, my focus scattered. Then, one day, I decided to exclude English from my daily study routine. I filled it with reading instead. As I halted my English learning, the wings of reading unfurled.

I left my job and embarked on a dedicated study of reading.

The library is a space where the soul dances [Image source: Pixabay]

To be honest, it wasn't so much about studying as it was about meeting ancient sages. Our conversations were truly enjoyable. The words of sages are always serene. And within that serenity lays profound wisdom, which is truly pleasing.

I found pleasure in meeting Socrates, Aristotle, Plato, Cicero, Marcus Aurelius, Ralph Waldo Emerson, Confucius, Mencius, Zhuangzi, Laozi, Yulgok Yi I, and Toegye Yi Hwang. Every morning, I packed my lunch and headed to the nearby library early in the morning. By 6:00 p.m., I would return home with a stack the books from the sages.

As I read, if I grew drowsy, I used the books as a makeshift pillow and dozed off. When I wanted to catch a breather while reading, I'd step outside and lay down on the pavilion's bench to read among the trees. The sunlight was always a gentle companion, and when it accompanied my reading, the words became clearer. My eyes felt refreshed. The path within the letters opened up.

This was the time when I read from the moment I opened my eyes in the morning to the moment I fell asleep at night—even in the restroom. It was impossible to put down whatever book I was reading.

Among the eight great Tang and Song Dynasty writers who admired Han Yu's sentences, Gu Yangsu is well-known for his 'three lots (三多)'. He mentioned three secrets to writing well: 'Read a lot (多讀)', 'Write a lot (多作)', and 'Think a lot (多常量)'. Can it get any clearer than this?

He named three places as the best spots for studying. First, on the bed. Second, on horseback. And third, on the toilet. He considered the time before sleeping, transition times, and even time in the restroom as excellent places for study, which shows his deep passion for reading. Indeed, he was referring to every bit of time that wasn't dedicated to daily routine.

Reading is not confined to a set time.

Ancient sages said reading was not just limited to books. They believed that all things in the world are a book as we learn from all things around us. Our lives themselves are a form of storytelling. They encompass the organizations we belong to, the people we meet, and everything we experience. Our lives go beyond seeing and hearing to engaging all our senses, and reading helps us closely observe the world around us.

In the depth of reading, the focus should always be on the heart. The heart is like the unseen roots of a tree. Since the heart is at the core of everything, we should ensure it's content. Reading takes care of both the mind and the heart. Reading enlivens the heart. However, we must remember that even more important than the heart on its own is physical health. By moving around and keeping active between and while reading, we care for our both physical health and our heart.

Just as all things are seen in mirrors, we must also constantly examine the mirror of our hearts.

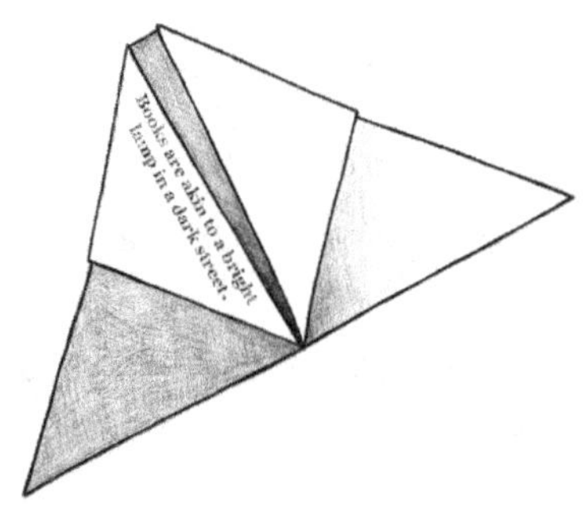

Books Are Akin to a Bright Lamp in a Dark Street

Reading Is Like Growing Bamboo

After spending five years deep underground, bamboo finally emerges. What was it doing beneath the ground during those five years? The underground roots of bamboo spread horizontally. This means that each bamboo is connected to the others, rather than having individual roots, like how we stand shoulder to shoulder with friends.

Reading connects us like the roots of bamboo, and also like the growth of the bamboo, while reading, changes may not be readily apparent, leading to doubt about the act of reading. However, we must believe in the power of books.

After five years, the bamboo shoots that were connected underground surge in unison. How astonishing this phenomenon is! When the bamboo finally emerges, how fast does it grow? There are instances where it grows over one meter in a day, which is truly remarkable.

It's said that tremendous energy is expended for rapid growth. Bamboo holds this energy within itself, and reading is no different. It might seem slow, but when the time is right, the benefits shoots up.

But where do the energies of all these books head to?

A bamboo forest resembles the 'forest of books' [Image source: Pixabay]

I visited Damyang Bamboo Forest.

How could a forest be so beautiful? I got to see the straight and graceful bends of bamboo. The rustling leaves and the way the wind danced with them left a lasting impression. How could it embody both straightness and gentleness?

Maintaining a consistent interval, the bamboo stalks stood tall as if they were tickling the neck of the clouds. The tall and slender stems moved gracefully as a whole, and I wondered if their roots were strong. I grasped one thick bamboo stalk and shook it. I was amazed by the strength of its roots, though it makes sense since each was like a companion to the others through the underground connections.

As my curiosity about bamboo developed, I learned that there's a period of stillness for growth and growth elements existed within such stillness. This concept applies to our rest, too. For those who have been filling up something too much, emptiness might mean rest. Conversely, for those who have been unable to fill what they intended, fulfillment might mean rest. Rest is both. In essence, fulfillment and emptiness are one.

So, how can we spend our own times segments?

Through the course of life, we can't always avoid fluctuations. When passing through a dark tunnel, we must always remember there's an end to it where light will return.

One day, everyone was driving cautiously through a heavy rain with their hazard lights on. Even the fastest windshield wiper setting wasn't enough to help see the road ahead, so we all proceeded carefully. After a while, we entered a tunnel. Inside the tunnel, the rain vanished and tranquility filled the space. As we exited the tunnel, the rain—as strong as ever—resumed, obscuring our vision. Yet, having briefly experienced tranquility within the tunnel, it made the storm a bit more bearable.

The tunnel didn't offer darkness; it offered reprieve.

The tunnel isn't darkness; it's a journey with the mountains [Image source: Pixabay]

Encountering a tunnel in life means striving to walk the path we desire. Haven't mountains been pierced to create a way, an easy shortcut for us?

While passing through the tunnel, we should look up at the mountain and the trees. Our vision should encompass not just one direction, but all around us, in every dimension. Just like bamboo growth segments, sometimes pausing for a moment is a way forward. Just as the idiom 'a bright lamp in a dark street' suggests, we must always recognize that there is light within the darkness.

And that light is none other than books. They are a flame that never goes out.

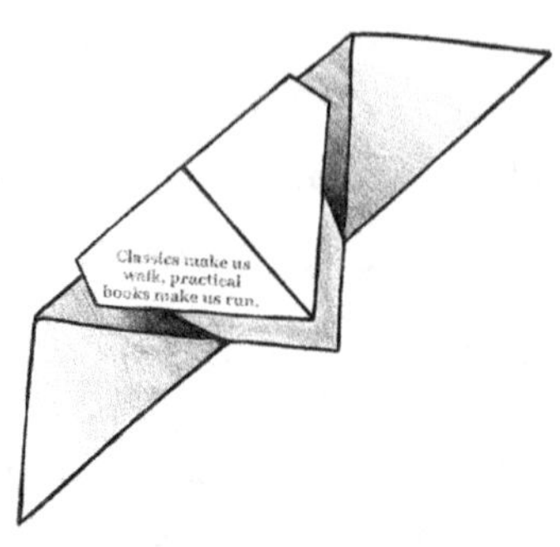

Classics Make Us Walk,
Practical Books Make Us Run

Life's path isn't meant to be only walked or only run. Walking and running, then running and walking—isn't that our life journey?

Classics say:

Why rush along the path of life so?
Take a moment to admire the scenery outside.
The beauty of nature;
it awaits you.

Yet within your eyes,
only other things are reflected.

Practical books say:

Life is at most, 120 years perhaps.
In the finiteness of life,
it's not a time for walking.

There is no time to admire the scenery.
You must sprint toward your destination.

After running, there will be time to walk.
Isn't it not the time to run now?

Reading only classics isn't enough, nor is reading only modern books. It's the harmony between classics and practical books that matters.

Classics are like a tree's roots, and practical books are like its trunk. Just as the life of a tree is determined by its roots, so too must we care for them. With strong roots, the trunk can grow, just as with strong roots, leaves can sprout. With strong roots, branches can extend, and with strong roots, fruits can be borne.

This is how important classics are in the world of books. Yet, if we only read classics, it's like listening only to classical music. Isn't there also opera, pop, jazz, or rock? There are countless genres of music, and the genres of books and music are quite similar. Mixing your favorite music genres into classical music brings rhythm to life.

If you haven't yet encountered classics, there's no need to worry. Once you step into the world of books, you'll inevitably meet them. Reading classics is as comforting as listening to classical music—it's akin to the feeling of a child resting in its mother's womb.

Books are protective clothing for me.
Books are nourishment that fattens my mind.
Books are the home where I comfortably dwell.

I wish to encounter a variety of books regardless of genre. However, humanities classics are must-reads. Not encountering humanities classics in our lives is like never having tasted the world's most exquisite and delicious dish.

When reading becomes a habit in life, I hope you savor the sweet taste and rich flavor of the classics to the fullest.

The taste of classic books
is like the world's finest cuisine.

Sail through the sea of books,
and you shall encounter the classics.

No need to rush,
for when the time is right, they'll come.

The subtle aroma of the dish
reaches your nose first.

When you encounter the cuisine of classics,
treasure and savor it.

The profound flavor of classics
is a delicacy of the world.

If you feel that your current life is moving too fast, it's time to meet the classics. Classics have the ability to slow life down. On the other hand, if you feel your life is moving too slowly, it's time to read practical books. Practical books can accelerate life.

In the harmony between slowness and speed, you'll find your own appropriate balance.

Choosing a book is like choosing clothes

When you try them on, your thoughts become simple [Image source: Pixabay]

Among your own books published each year, which should you choose? Recommending books is a delicate task. How about experiencing the fun of choosing for yourself rather than books that have been recommended to you?

Choosing a book is like choosing clothes. Is it the right size for your body? Does the color suit you? Is the design what you desire? Is the fabric of good quality? Selecting clothes can be a challenging task. Judging only by sight might not give you a clear sense. However, what if you try them on? When you actually put on the clothes, you'll come to know if it suits you or not. The same goes for books. You only truly know if it's the right book for you when you taste it.

Just as you need to taste food to truly understand its flavor, you need to taste books to appreciate them. The more you taste, the more you become a connoisseur; the more you read, the more you become a reader.

The more you wear clothes, the better you become at choosing them. The more you read books, the better you become at choosing them.

Choosing well means satisfying yourself. If you find it difficult to choose a book, narrow down your thoughts. What nutrients do you need right now? What nutrients might our organization need right now? The book that provides the nutrients you need might be the book you're looking for. The book that can answer your current questions is the book you should choose. If the book complements your concerns and provides hints on your concerns, a chemical reaction might occur within you. You gain the power to resolve your concerns on your own. Books are fascinating in that even if a particular book doesn't seem to fit you now, you never know when it will become relevant.

That's why books should be read at all times.

If a sentence in the book catches your attention upon opening it, take it home before settling for a book that was recommended to you or a bestselling book. The more captivating sentences you encounter, the more likely they match your taste. Opening a book and traversing the forest is akin to tasting food at a sampling stand. Just as you taste food and decide to buy it if it suits your palate, books work the same way. A book that suits you will naturally lead you to the next one.

Still finding it difficult to choose a book? Consider checking out the NBIC (NEXT BIG IDEA CLUB) app. Listening to insights from remarkable authors directly can greatly assist you in making choices.

Once you've chosen a book you like, explore books within books. As one book leads to another, and another to yet another, it's like pulling out strings of fresh potatoes from a potato field. The books quoted within another book tend to share similar themes, so there's a high likelihood they have related subjects. Think of this system as the original social media and video platform algorithms.

By following the trail of quotes from one book to another, you might find that your concerns have been resolved along the way.

Books reflect who I am. The themes of the books I've read mirror my areas of interest. If you're unsure about yourself, reviewing the titles of books you've read could be a method to selecting what to read too. By following the path of the books you've already finished, you might encounter your true self.

If you like an author, take the time to explore their other works. You can check the books introduced in their profile or those mentioned in the back flap.

Still having trouble? If you've found a book you like, take note of the publisher. You can visit their website or search for it online if you plan to make an online purchase. If you liked one book, the chances are high that you'll like other books from the same source. As your reading volume increases, you'll come to recognize more publishers, and you'll notice the distinctive features of each publisher.

Furthermore, when it comes to reading, it's also beneficial to explore your areas of interest and expand beyond your primary topics.

Peter Drucker's reading approach involved gradually expanding into different fields. Every three to four years, he shifted his focus. This resulted in a broad and comprehensive knowledge base, and he became an insightful management consultant known as the 'Father of Modern Management.'

You could delve deeply into one subject or expand your horizons to diverse fields. There's no definitive reading method, so just get started with it. Once you begin, the next steps will become clearer.

One important thing to keep in mind when reading is to avoid reading analytically. Reading analytically can hinder the merging of yourself with the book. Reading is a meeting with the author. A meeting is a conversation. It's about listening to the author's story and sharing your own thoughts.

When analysis is necessary, I recommend that you taste the book first and then read it again.

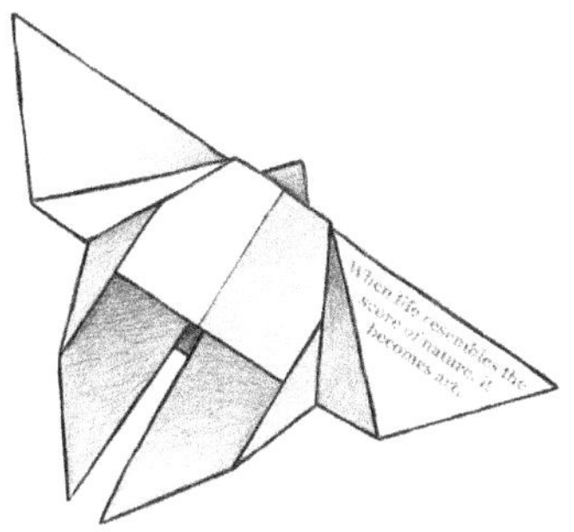

Life becomes art when we resemble nature's musical score

The reason for studying is to understand human beings. To understand human beings, you must first understand yourself. Understanding yourself begins with recognizing your shortcomings. Second, it involves knowing your beauty. You need to know the beauty within yourself to comprehend the beauty in others. Shortcomings give rise to learning, and beauty gives rise to love.

Is there another lover as great as nature? As we gradually come to understand the nature lover, our lives turn into art.

Our Lives, Resembling Nature

Nature is never the same across the seasons.
The autumnal tinting is not the same as the previous year.
What about the tree rings?
Different works are carved each year.

Some years, straight lines are drawn.
Some years, bent lines are drawn.
Straightness and curvature combine,
creating four seasons and the pattern of life.

Spring, summer, autumn, winter.

The seasons of life are no different.
No one escapes the passage of time.
Why wouldn't autumn come into my life?
Why wouldn't spring come into my life?

When spring comes, summer follows.
When summer comes, autumn arrives.
When autumn comes, winter approaches.
Let's prepare and embrace it.

Upon the arrival of winter,
pure white snow covers love.
The life of humans, the life of nature,
they truly resemble each other.

What is studying? The greatest study in life is the study of understanding oneself. To understand ourselves, we need the aid of a valuable tool: books. Books are like mirrors reflecting our inner selves. It would be great if we could see our hearts in a mirror, but that's not possible. Books act as a tool to illuminate our heart.

Let us study together, accompanied by books and nature.

There are no same works in this world. Every second, a different piece of work is produced. The wildflowers in the field work the same way. They seem still but move quietly. That's why nature is always vibrant.

What about our lives? Life requires rhythm. Let's place notes evenly on the stage of life. Quarter notes (♩), eighth notes (♪, ♫), and occasionally even sixteenth notes (♬) could be thrown in. Rhythm makes our lives lively.

When writing the score of life, remember this: there are as many rests as there are notes. You'll run out of breath in a score without rests. The beauty of music lies within the rests.

The score that most resembles nature is children [Image source: Pixabay]

If there were too many rests in my life, I would introduce fast-tempo notes to bring balance. If my life's tempo was too rapid, I would slow down the beats. We are the conductors of the score that plays out our lives. Nature does not get bored. The absence of boredom is due to the skillful arrangement of notes and rests. To write a score that suits my life, I must know myself well. Knowing myself leads to satisfaction.

To be able to freely write the score I desire, books are essential.

Beauty Learned From Water

Water is responsible for cleansing all things. It cleanses dirt and muck, and it supplies the essence of life. How can we express the beauty of water?

I had always been amazed by the pebbles on the seashore. How did water develop the skill to shape the sharp edges so smoothly and roundly? While gently stroking the subject, water reveals its true beauty without causing harm, as if whispering, "This is your true beauty." So I was surprised when Professor Yoo Yeongman, a knowledge ecologist from Hanyang University, mentioned pebbles during our interview. He then introduced the concept of "bojagi," a traditional Korean wrapping cloth.

Bojagi, unlike a bag, places the other at the center, not oneself. It symbolizes the virtue of humbly embracing and lowering oneself to accommodate others. It was a time when I gained a new perspective on the wonders of bojagi. He mentioned that water is similar in this aspect.

So, what is the enchanting beauty of water? Let's think for a moment.

The veteran of Earth's journeys is water [Image Source: Pixabay]

Water gently rises, even in the highest and steepest canyons. No matter how rough and pointed the rocks it encounters, water wraps them softly. Its gentleness amazes its recipients. It rises as vapor, reaching up to the sky. It becomes one with the clouds, lingering for a while, and then descends again. As raindrops, it embraces all things and moistens the earth. The water that bathes and embraces is not wasted; it tenderly moistens the earth.

Water doesn't adhere to a fixed path. There's no predetermined route. It always makes choices based on the situation. If there is no path, it creates one, while always keeping its ultimate destination, the sea, in mind. It knows when to pause temporarily, such as when the earth freezes during a cold spell. But whenever an opportunity arises, it keeps moving forward without hesitation. Water doesn't miss small chances. It travels to numerous places on Earth, and while traveling, when it meets other streams of water, it merges smoothly. Then, it becomes part of a larger current. Even as it progresses, if the paths diverge, each stream follows its own course. They may meet again after following their separate paths.

Water is always gentle. No matter how high it travels, it knows its place is ultimately on the ground. Its gaze is upward, but it always keeps an eye below. This humility is the essence of water. Above all, the greatest beauty of water lies in its authenticity. It adjusts to others while staying true to itself—maintaining its core essence.

A happy life is an authentic life. If I am not true to myself, no matter what I have, I will always feel empty. All things are most beautiful when they are authentic. A rose is most beautiful when it is being a rose, and a forsythia is most beautiful when it is being a forsythia.

A thorn does not belong on a forsythia; it belongs on a rose, just as water is most beautiful when it is purely itself.

So, where do we find authenticity?

How about giving myself the gift of the world of books? Reading is a process of seeking authenticity and finding one's self. Conversation with books is the flowery scent of communication. If you smell the flower, you can find your flower.

Only I can know what I am. No one can replace me. No matter what I do, being myself is the most original and artistic.

How can the sheet music of our lives be the same? How can the colors of life be the same? The only person who can play the score of your life is yourself. Instead of comparing myself to anyone else, let's draw as just me. When nature's score enters our lives, our lives become art. How could the score of life be the same for everyone? How could the tinting of life be identical?

Only I can play the score of my life. It should not be about comparing ourselves with others; it should be about being authentically me.

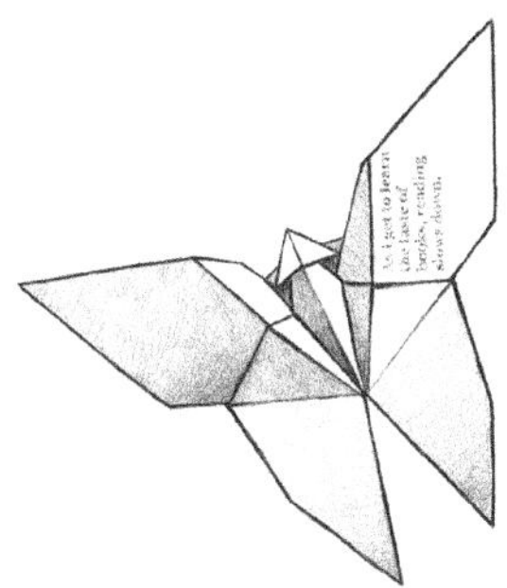

As I Learn the Taste of Books, Reading Slows Down

How much time does it take to read a single book? While it might feel like speed picks up as you proceed, reading slows down over time. Discovering the deep flavor of a book is like taking a leisurely walk through a forest of words rather than a race. There are moments of pausing and moments of moving forward. It's akin to encountering a magnificent spot during a journey and absorbing the breathtaking scenery as you linger for a while. The nutrients and energy from that experience become a part of your body—like blood and muscles.

Books back in the day included a stamped postcard between the very last pages. It would ask you to share your thoughts with the publisher. How did you find the book? During the time when reading was pure delight, I wrote a note on the postcards and sent them.

"It felt like picking up precious gems," I wrote.

Once, my entry was chosen, and I received another book as a gift. I remember savoring that gifted book just as deliciously. While the postcard that used to grace the final pages of books has since disappeared, it remains a cherished memory. It was like encountering a flag at the summit after climbing a mountain while relishing the surrounding scenery. Now, I leave a few lines of my impressions on the last page of the book in place of the postcard.

Especially when reading old works, I can't help but be amazed. How could ten vowels and fourteen consonants come together to create such combinations of words? The infinite soaring of letters astounds me, over and over again.

The writing of the past is like classical music. It possesses calmness and elegance, a gentle strength, and above all, a profound serenity. Even as time passes, and I revisit those writings, their taste remains pure and crisp. In fact, the taste matures over time. That's the taste of the classics, the taste of books.

Some pieces of writing feel like drawing water from the depths of the earth, deep and profound. Others feel like lively fish in a pond, playfully skipping on the surface. Some books are like watching a grand opera, while others are so exquisite, I want to savor them bit by bit so as not to waste them.

The Most Beautiful Taste of Writing: Yi Deok-mu and the Bukhak Pragmatists

I followed sentences, tracing the figures as I read. When the sentences called me, I followed the figures they portrayed.

After two decades of reading, I had the chance to meet a figure in my imagination. It was the enchanting sentences that led me. It was none other than Yi Deok-mu, the person who self-deprecatingly referred to himself as a fool who only read books. The person who sold his cherished copy of *Mencius* to appease hunger when there was no food to eat. The person who covered himself with a thin blanket of *Book of*

Han and shielded himself from the wind with the pages of *The Analects of Confucius.* The person who diligently transcribed the text of a rare book he borrowed. He wrote in minute handwriting to save paper.

Why had he been so poor? He was a 'seoja'. In those times, a soeja referred to the child of a concubine. People of seoja origin faced many restrictions in society. Poverty and concerns about meals were a constant fate. Yet, an opportunity presented itself to him. In the year 1778, at the age of thirty-eight, Yi Deok-mu had a chance to step out into the world, and he, too, found his purpose. He was appointed as an envoy to China, and in the following year, in 1779, he got into the government service.

Yi Deok-mu's friend, Bak Jega, along with Yu Deuk Gong and Seo Ri Su, were granted positions as librarians at Gyujanggak Library. Gyujanggak Library was a significant academic research institution that would contribute to the advancement of Joseon's scholarly endeavors, serving as the royal library.

How delighted I had been! Isn't every human meant for a purpose? The happiest moments come when we live according to our calling because this calling molds us into our true selves. A life that is uniquely ours is a happy life.

Yi Deok-mu, too, concluded his life according to his chosen calling. Constantly engaged in the pursuit of reading, he honed his potential, unsure of when he might be called upon to serve. If he had blamed his social status and stopped reading, what might have become of him?

If I were to choose the purest writing from all I've read, I would choose that of Yi Deok-mu. His writing is like pristine water that has passed through thousands of years of filtration atop a lofty mountain peak, seemingly reaching the sky. Delicate tea leaves were added to that water and brewed once more. What could possibly compare to the clear taste of his writing?

When I'm taken aback by archaic writing, translated works become a guiding light. Writing is always a bountiful harvest. The field of writing is perpetually a field of gold. The vibrant yellow "wheat of words" is always a welcoming sight.

The Greatest Pleasure of Discovering Life Books

The book I truly savored each bite of was Yulgok Yi I's, *Sunghakjipyo*. Despite its thickness, with over 600 pages, as I turned the pages, the remaining ones always left me yearning for more. As the remaining chapters dwindled, my sense of longing grew. It's like when you're checking how much time is remaining in a beautiful movie, only to realize that time keeps slipping away. Your sense of yearning grows stronger.

After meeting Yi Deok-mu, I pondered. Did I read books so intently to meet figures like him? Did I read so much to meet the Bukhak Pragmatists, including the esteemed Yeonam Bak Jiwon and Dasan Jeong Yak-yong?

It was only after meeting these figures that I found solace in the interludes of reading.

If I were to select two books from my life, I would choose *The Analects of Confucius* and *Sunghakjipyo*. Perhaps it's because I encountered them in my early thirties. That was before I learned about Yi Deok-mu. However, after meeting Yi Deok-mu, who had read over a thousand books, I discovered that he, too, held *Sunghakjipyo* in high regard.

I was delighted by a sense of resonance. It's such a joy that two people, living nearly 300 years apart can find communion through their life's books. Why not become friends with someone from the past?

Yi Deok-mu also recommended these two books: *Bangyesurok* by Yu Hyeongwon and *Dongui Bogam* by Heo Jun.

In addition to Confucius's *Analects* and Yi I's *Sunghakjipyo*, if I were to add one more book, it would be Marcus Aurelius's *Meditations*.

The taste changes as I read. The richness of a hearty broth is truly splendid. While books remain the same, as we change, the taste changes alongside. Even as time flows, the flavor of authenticity remains unwavering. All three of these books are highly recommended for leaders in our workplaces.

It would be wonderful to encounter these books as you deepen your understanding of the taste of reading. Though I fear that meeting them too early might prevent you from savoring the true flavor of the books, for they are books we should cherish and chew on carefully.

The pleasure of discovering one's life book will undoubtedly be the greatest gift to our lives. They will become cherished companions for a lifetime, true friends who always support and stand by us. No matter how high the wall, with a staircase of books, we can overcome it. As the barriers rise, so do the steps, allowing us to appreciate the panoramic view from the summit. The masters within the books guide us, step by step. It's because of them that we can emit our own light.

It's because of them that I can truly be me.

TAKING A BREAK:

RESEARCH IMMERSION, THE STARTING POINT OF CREATIVE RESEARCH, by Professor Hwang Nongmun (Seoul National University)

Source: KIRD R&D HRD RESEARCH & FIELD VO1.1

- Professional Development of S&T Researchers

Why Should We Immerse Ourselves in Research?

The motivation for research immersion can be categorized into external and internal factors. The environment at your workplace may or may not be conducive to research immersion. Since external factors often lie beyond our control, let's consider internal factors that are within our control.

If there's a reason for me to immerse myself, what might that be? The reason is evident: it's due to the ephemeral nature of life. The decision to create a single masterpiece from the unique opportunity of life or to let it fade away as formless mist rests solely with oneself.

I didn't exist in the distant past, and I won't exist in the far future. I'm merely here for a brief moment. In other words, I am inevitably destined to die someday. What can I do about this fated death? What can I do to resist it?

The time I am alive is a singular opportunity, and whether I make the most of this opportunity or not is up to me. In the face of the impending death that slowly approaches, the best I can do is live the most life-affirming life while I'm alive. Rather than a life that is barely distinguishable from death, a life where I am merely existing, I must live a life that is least like death. It should be a life brimming with vibrancy and the joy of living, a life where I maximize every ability I possess, no matter how small. Because the fact of being alive is my one and only chance. This is why I choose to immerse myself.

As researchers, we should value our precious and singular lives, so we should strive to engage in research that is both significant and far-reaching. It would be even better if we perceive our research as something that we're willing to trade with our lives. Of course, the perceived value is relative. Therefore, even a topic that once had been unfamiliar and uninteresting at the outset of our research can become a source of immersion, igniting our lives. It is in such moments that we might even perceive a sense of sanctity, feeling that it is valuable enough to trade without lives.

How to Become Immersed in Research

So, how can one become immersed in research? How can I ignite my life as a researcher? We must become deeply absorbed in the critical issues related to our research, thinking about them day and night. Whether walking along the road, driving, eating, or showering, our minds should be focused on these problems. Don't be discouraged or shaken by a lack of progress. Instead, continue thinking about these matters relentlessly. Even if there's no apparent progress, persistent contemplation will lead you closer to the core of the problem. Over time, you will reach a heightened state of immersion where only the problem and you exist in consciousness.

The process of raising immersion levels can be likened to kindling a fire. Depending on the research topic or mindset, it may be difficult for the fire to ignite at first. However, once you reach a state of deep immersion and the fire is ignited, it will naturally start to burn. From that point onward, you need not exert much effort. Your curiosity and passion for the problem will grow so much, it will automatically generate the best driving force.

After completing my doctoral degree, I began working as a senior researcher at the Korea Research Institute of Standards and Science. I was assigned a research project on low-pressure diamonds. This topic was neither within my field of expertise nor of personal interest. The principal investigator who had secured research funding for this project had been appointed to a university, leaving someone else to carry out the project, who turned out to be me.

For a researcher, this is the worst-case scenario. Despite the miserable situation, I decided to immerse myself in the most crucial aspect of the project, thinking that it would do me more harm than good if I stayed miserable. I intentionally focused my thoughts solely on the relevant issues of the research day and night.

Initially, I thought a week would be enough to understand the experiment results, only to find it more perplexing the longer I thought about it. I spent weeks immersing myself in related literature and experiments, yet I still couldn't make sense of it. I didn't want to give up. Thinking, *we'll see who wins*, I persevered.

It wasn't a moderate effort. I poured my heart and soul into it, thinking about the problem day and night, as if my life depended on it. Yet, for several months, there was no progress.

Anger started to build up. It felt as though the problem had punched me in the face when I was just going on with my life. The deeply suppressed instinctive aggressiveness within me emerged. I thought to myself, *hey, you! You picked a fight with me, and you're going down with me!* I was determined to fight to the end.

I can confidently say that at that time, even if someone had held a knife to my throat and threatened me to work even harder than I was doing then, I couldn't have given any more effort.

The results obtained from experiments can never deviate from the laws of nature. In this regard, solving a problem is akin to catching a rat trapped inside a jar. However, imagine that the rat remains uncaptured for several months. It took a year and a half to find a clear answer. The reason it took so long was that the textbooks that explained the growth of thin membranes had been wrong.

These textbooks described that thin membranes grow at an atomic scale, and I had believed them. This phenomenon is known as **classical crystallization**. However, what I discovered was that when charged* nanoparticles appear in the air, they create diamonds on a silicon substrate and soot on an iron plate. This phenomenon is referred to as **non-classical crystallization**.

This discovery became one of my most significant achievements. I presented over a hundred research papers related to this topic and compiled them into a book titled *Non-Classical Crystallization of*

Thin Films and Nanostructures in CVD and PVD Processes, which was published by Springer in 2016.

***A phenomenon where particles are charged electrically**

Allow me to introduce an excerpt from the book *Immersion*, which was published in 2007, based on the experience I solved the problem.

It was 1 a.m. I woke up in the middle of the night without fail. As consciousness returned, I was already thinking about the problem. For the past year and a half, this problem had occupied my mind entirely. Falling asleep while contemplating the problem and waking up to the same thoughts had become a routine. I knew this would continue until the problem was resolved.

Ideas that come to mind upon waking are easily forgotten if not recorded. So, I had to get up from my bed to promptly write them down in my notebook. Waking up was not difficult at all; perhaps it became a habit or it was because I went to bed early. It wasn't a forced awakening; it was as if my body naturally awoke itself.

In the tranquil early dawn, with all living things asleep, I felt like the sole existence in this vast universe, solely existing to think about this problem. This might be the pinnacle of human concentration. A deep sense of tranquility and happiness welled up from within.

Slightly excited, I paced the living room, continuing to ponder the problem. The quiet of dawn allowed ideas to flow continuously. The riddle felt as if it was on the verge of being solved yet remained unresolved. This enigmatic state persisted for over a year. The feeling that it could be solved at any moment and the sense that it was almost within grasp drove me crazy. Where did this unwavering expectation that I could definitely solve the problem come from? What was the basis for this daily, self-assured confidence? Perhaps my persistence in not letting go of this problem stemmed not just from the determination to solve it but from the hopeful anticipation that it would be solved soon and my conviction that I could indeed solve it.

The Principle Behind the Formation of Creative Ideas in an Immersive State

Ordinarily, creative ideas are not easily obtained. However, during my seven years of tenure at the Korea Research Institute of Standards and Science, I experienced the pinnacle of immersion where miraculous and creative ideas flowed continuously. I interpreted my experiences based on neuroscience knowledge and detailed the principles behind the generation of creative ideas in my books *Immersion* and *Immersion: A Second Story*. The core principle can be summarized as follows:

Our brain is involved in both storing and retrieving memories. However, the ability to store memories is exceptionally high when we are awake but significantly reduced during sleep. In simple terms, the ability to store memories is close to that of a genius during the day but drops to the level of an imbecile during sleep. This is because the production of neurotransmitters such as dopamine, serotonin, and norepinephrine, which are essential for short-term memory storage, is high during the day when we are awake, but it decreases significantly during our sleep.

Acetylcholine[*] is a neurotransmitter associated with memory retrieval. Acetylcholine increases during sleep, reaching its peak during REM[**] (rapid eye movement) sleep. Additionally, when we fall asleep, the prefrontal cortex becomes inactive, and the network responsible for storing representations of suppressed memories in the prefrontal cortex becomes active. The deactivation of the prefrontal cortex and the increase in acetylcholine allow deeper access to the subconscious, making it easier to retrieve long-term memories stored there. In other words, when we fall asleep, the retrieval ability of long-term memories becomes significantly heightened.

Since creative ideas are connected to the retrieval of long-term memories related to solving a problem, it is evident that creativity will be enhanced during sleep.

Therefore, when we fall asleep every night, the retrieval ability of long-term memories becomes heightened, giving us a brain that can produce creative ideas like a genius. However, there is a catch. When we fall asleep, the prefrontal cortex becomes inactive, resulting in a loss of problem awareness. Consequently, we are unable to utilize the brain's genius capacity. Despite experiencing the genius brain connected to creativity every night, we can't use it effectively.

**Neurotransmitter involved in memory regulation or inducing muscle contraction*

***A stage of sleep characterized by the eyes moving quickly several times. This stage is also known as paradoxical sleep because despite being asleep, the brainwave pattern resembles wakefulness.*

So, how can we utilize the creative brain enhanced during sleep? To achieve this, one must continue thinking about the problem even while asleep. In other words, one must enter a state of lucid sleep. To create such a state, one needs to engage in immersive thinking of the problem without taking a break for several days.

Slow thinking involves thinking about a given problem without a pause, as if one is leisurely contemplating in a relaxed state. It's a thinking method in which the focus is on the process itself rather than fixating on the outcome. Slow thinking is also the most powerful engine for increasing immersion, as it allows prolonged thinking without exhaustion. By using slow thinking to increase immersion, individuals can deeply engage in their work or research and bring forth their best abilities.

Science and technology are essential assets for responding to rapid future changes and are a critical survival strategy for the Republic of Korea, which lacks natural resources. In recent times, the importance of interdisciplinary collaboration in the field of science and technology has grown, and there is a need for voluntary learning activities to develop into creative and interdisciplinary researchers.

Through immersion, I hope researchers can turn their responsibilities into tasks they enjoy and elevate the completeness of their limited lives through fulfilling pursuits.

I ATTAINED – EYES TO SEE BEAUTY

Books guide us beyond inner beauty to eyes
that can see the beauty of all things

Life's Experiences Are
Like Paint Tubes

I paint life with the brush of 'me'. How many different paint tubes do I have? Diverse colors come together to paint a picture of one's life. The gift of twenty-four hours a day is the same for everyone. Within those hours, what do I allocate the most time to?

Let us pay attention to the quantity, density, and frequency of time. The more quantity, the stronger the density, and the higher the frequency, the more life's painting leans toward those directions. It becomes the central pattern of the painting of life.

So, what kind of picture am I painting with the brush called life? What is the central pattern of my life? It encompasses the time spent on actions and thoughts. When painting, there is no reason to rush. Life's painting also includes moments of stillness.

Each of our experiences is a process of creating a paint tube. These paints come together to complete a picture. Experiences come together to complete a life. Life isn't just one brush. In fact, we have multiple brushes, as the painting of life requires a variety of tools.

In my life, I can utilize both large and small brushes. Consider where to use the large brushes and where to use the small ones, thinking about importance and priorities. The picture of my life can only be completed by me. If there are parts of the picture that I want to change while painting, I can always make modifications.

Isn't there white paint in the paint tubes of life? White paint is a gift given from the moment of birth. It's not just any color; it's a magical color. Regardless of the colors used in the painting, this paint has the ability to turn everything white. If I want to, I can start over on a fresh canvas of white paint.

There is not just a single brush of life [Image source: Pixabay]

Common Traits of Those Who Achieve Their Dreams

First, they have clear dreams. Second, they believe. If they can vividly paint their dreams and believe in themselves, those dreams will come true. It's just a matter of timing; they will be fulfilled eventually.

Another common trait among those who achieve their dreams is that they have endured solitude. Can cherry blossoms be found on a winter mountain? It's challenging. Everyone is the same in this regard. Only when the flowers bloom can we recognize them as cherry blossoms. Only a few people have the ability to recognize a tree without flowers. Instead of blaming the absence of companions who can help us achieve our dreams, what if we cultivate the ability to recognize trees that haven't blossomed yet?

The fourth common trait of dream achievers is positivity. They possess the power of positivity. They see positivity in every situation rather than negativity. This is why they constantly seek to learn. Learning is concealed within strengths, not weaknesses. The power of positivity allows them to quickly recognize strengths and offer praise. This is why they emit a fragrance. A pleasant fragrance gathers people because the energy of happiness is embedded within it.

The fifth common trait shared among dream achievers is good habits. They quickly make other people's good habits their own and swiftly adopt other people's strengths. They are masters of emulation. They excel at immediately making good things their own. The key word here is 'immediately'. They choose the present rather than procrastinating. Good habits include the habit of reading books. They always keep books close by.

These five common traits can be summarized in a single word. Self-esteem.

The greatest characteristic of dream achievers is having high self-esteem, which allows them to view the journey of their dreams through the lens of happiness. Ultimately, this feeling of happiness guides them towards their dreams. If the outlining color of happiness is self-esteem, then reading is the brush that colors happiness.

Let's embark on the journey of dreams with books.

If I smile, the organization will smile too [Image source: Pixabay]

Dreams are essential not only for individuals but also for organizations. The indispensable education for any organization is self-esteem education. This is because self-esteem serves as the foundation for both individual and organizational growth.

Organizations with high self-esteem achieve exceptional results. Self-esteem is akin to the roots of a tree. When the roots are strong, the tree grows. So does the organization.

Individuals and organizations are not separate. When individuals grow, organizations grow, and when organizations grow, individuals also grow. This relationship is similar to that of a needle and thread.

The needle must be smooth to avoid damaging the fabric, while the thread must be strong to ensure longevity. However, a needle alone or thread alone cannot fulfill their roles. It is the collaboration between the needle and thread that produces the achievements of the organization. A beautiful dress is created by the collaboration of needle and thread.

Does our organization have a goal? Does it have a dream? An organization's dreams should be shared with its employees. If a company is the moon, its employees should not forget that they are the stars.

There is an old Korean saying, 'gwasukcheorak (과숙체락)', which means 'when a cucumber is ripe, it falls on its own'. This saying signifies that when the right time comes, things will happen naturally.

Personal dreams and organizational dreams are ultimately realized.

If the time has not yet come to achieve your dream, it's not the right time. You must wait for the right time. Believe in yourself and continue forward through learning. Isn't there a saying that water flows down only when it fills up the hollow areas?

Books can assist in achieving dreams. With books, both personal and organizational dreams can be fulfilled. The mentors within books can become your dream companions. The teacher in the book will become your dream buddy. If you continue talking with your dream friend, you will eventually find yourself reaching your dream.

You should enjoy the process of reading a book. You must enjoy the process of dreaming. If you enjoy it, you will soon become what you dreamed of.

The Sun Possesses Gentleness, While the Moon Possesses Brilliance

In any given organization, if there is a sun, there must also be a moon. It's not enough to have only one. The sun's gentleness and the moon's brilliance must come together. It's the harmony between them that makes day and night beautiful.

Are there individuals who possess the qualities of the sun? Are there individuals who possess the qualities of the moon? When the harmony of the sun and the moon is achieved, the organization radiates depth and unique dynamics.

When forming an organization, one should think of creating a beautiful garden. How will the trees and flowers be harmoniously arranged? Where should they be placed to achieve the greatest beauty? In a beautiful garden, butterflies and birds gather.

What makes the rainbow beautiful?

If rainbows were not curved but straight, how would we have perceived them? There is always a curve hidden in beauty. It holds a gentle power. It holds the power of harmony.

The rainbow is held by a curve [Image source: Pixabay]

If our tongues were square, could we have blended various foods smoothly and harmoniously?

In an Organization, the Most Essential Power is the Power of Harmony

The greatest quality of a leader resides in their ability to create harmony. Nature can become a remarkable leader because it strives for harmony. The foundation of harmony begins with understanding what is 'precious'.

The first step in understanding preciousness is knowing the value of oneself, followed by recognizing the value of others. First, you must comprehend your own preciousness, and then recognize the preciousness of others. When you understand the preciousness and worth of yourself, harmony begins. Everything originates from oneself.

When the time comes, flowers bloom. Flowers never rush. When the time comes, they are dyed in colors. Trees never rush. They don't urge flowers to blossom upon the arrival of spring. They don't push leaves to become tinged with red when autumn comes. They understand that when the time comes, flowers bloom and leaves put on autumnal tints.

Isn't it more beautiful to have pauses in between blooms and falls? Forsythias bloom first, followed by cherry blossoms, then azaleas. How many trees and flowers come together in harmony to create a beautiful scene of autumn foliage? There, various plants from sunny and shady areas, as well as partial-shade plants, blend harmoniously. Together, they create a beautiful forest.

When a tree collapses, the others lend their shoulders. When a landslide occurs and roots are exposed, large rocks come closer to provide support. The mountain has not only flowers and trees but also animals, insects, rocks, and soil. It has the wind, sun, water, and the moon. Harmony brings forth a pleasant fragrance. Harmony creates a pleasing sight. Harmony produces beautiful sounds. Even the traveling clouds pause for a moment, captivated by the enchanting harmony.

Nature's ultimate skill is harmony [Image source: Pixabay]

Just as the sun possesses harmony and the moon possesses brilliance, how about we bring the beauty of nature into our organization? Nothing is insignificant. No person is without worth. When each individual is respected, an organization blossoms. It becomes a garden where butterflies dance, a place where happiness resides.

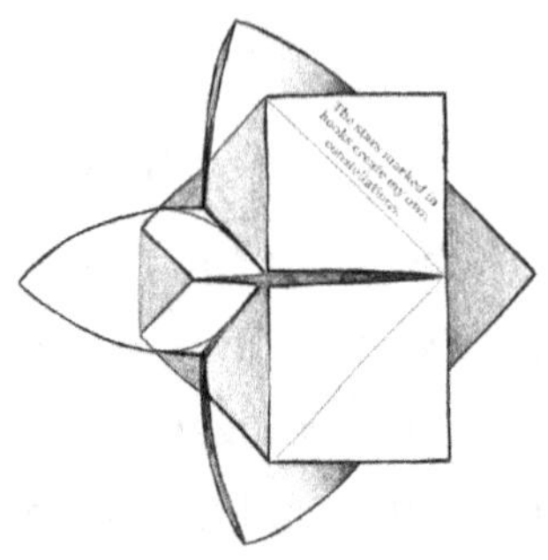

The Stars Marked in Books
Create My Own Constellations

How many stars have I marked in books until now? I underlined and put stars next to important sentences. The more important they were, the larger the stars. Little stars gathered to form a starry field, which turned into a galaxy. Soon after, it became the universe.

The stars within books create their own constellations and the universe of the heart carries stars. For readers, their very own universe always exists. In the vast expanse of space, they draw up their own constellations.

Encounter with Teachers and Friends

Reading is like climbing a mountain. It's as if you're walking on flat ground, encountering uphill paths, then walking on level ground again, and later encountering downhill slopes. After a while, you may find yourself lost at a crossroad. Paths might narrow or widen. Sometimes, rain falls, leaving the ground muddy. After pulling yourself together, you continue on the path. The sun gently envelops you, as if nothing happened.

Reading also encompasses a journey through all four seasons. Just as you climb a mountain in each season, there are also sceneries in the seasons of reading.

Dazzling green spring mountains.
The energy of growth in summer mountains.
The conception of life in autumn mountains.
Pure-hearted winter mountains.

After going through all four seasons,
I started seeing true friends.

Meeting old friends
with hearty laughter;
utter joy.

How noble is this.
How grateful I am.

Even if I lived just one day,
conversing with a golden friend
blooms my heart like a flower.
You are the flower in the book.

There are particular friends who hold a special place in my heart. They are the Bukhak Pragmatists and Dasan Jeong Yak-yong, as well as Yi Deok-mu, Bak Jega and Yeonam Bak Jiwon, the greatest scholars of the Joseon Dynasty, as introduced earlier in the book.

Is it because I encountered them after twenty years of reading? The afterglow of these remarkable friends particularly remains with me for a long time.

When I encountered the Bukhak Pragmatists, I just wanted to run to them without a second thought. Weren't they the very friends I had dreamed of? Isn't Dasan Jeong Yak-yong a true exemplar of a venerable teacher? If you want to know more about them, the Silhak Museum in Namyangju, Gyeonggi Province is the right place to visit. You'll get to see Dasan Jeong Yak-yong's birth house and even his tomb.

One of the greatest rewards of my reading journey was getting to meet true teachers and friends. Although they might be just book friends, they are flower friends to me. They are moon friends. They are star friends. The reason I regard them as exceptional teachers and friends is not solely because of their splendid accomplishments but because I saw fragrant flower gardens within the vast universe. It's because I saw shining star fields, twinkling and radiant. It was a beautiful and splendid landscape created by kind and noble hearts.

Portrait of Yeonam Bak Jiwon painted by his grandson Bak Jusu (1797-1801)

Source: Korean Wikipedia https://ko.wikipedia.org/wiki/박지원_(1737년)

Portrait of Dasan Jeong Yak-yong (1762-1836)

Source: Korean Wikipedia https://ko.wikipedia.org/wiki/정약용

Portrait of Bak Jega (1750-1805)

Source: Korean Wikipedia https://ko.wikipedia.org/wiki/박제가

When the grains of millet (a type of yellow grain) gather together, they become sticky and dense. Its when small things come together that they gain true strength.

By reading book after book, before you know it, you'll have reached a dense and sticky state. One star, another star, as you draw them one by one before you realize it, they've become a galaxy.

This field of stars is my heart. The stars painted in the book form constellations within my universe. What were once seemingly insignificant stars become a radiant constellation, illuminating the world with beautiful light.

Dasan Jeong Yak-yong's Approach to Reading

During his exile, Dasan Jeong Yak-yong had holes in his bones on three different occasions from intense writing activities, so the classics describe it. In Korea, Dasan Jeong Yak-yong is considered a great person and his anecdote is widely known. He learned from his father and pursued self-study through reading, becoming one of the most prolific writers since the invention of the Chinese characters. He compiled the thoughts of practical science of the late Joseon period and, above all, loved his people. Such feats are possible only through love.

Dasan's approach to reading consisted of three main principles: thorough reading, notes, and transcription (筆寫). When he encountered unfamiliar content, he would look up references, analyze, and read again. Whenever he came across enlightening passages, he made notes. Transcription involved selecting and transcribing only materials that contributed to his academic pursuits, essentially a form of transcription. Transcribing implies 'writing in imitation'.

Whenever you encounter a sentence that resonates with you, open your transcription notebook and write it down as it is. Later, when you revisit that notebook, you'll feel like you're strolling through a field of gold.

That's what it feels like.

It's similar to having a collection of favorite songs stored on a USB drive and listening to it while walking through beautiful scenery.

I, too, once engaged in transcribing while reading. I wrote down sentences in my transcription notebook, leaving several lines blank below each one. In those empty spaces, I jotted down my thoughts on that sentence.

As the volume of reading increases, so does the volume of thoughts. Your personal values start to solidify. As your reading volume expands, you might even feel as if you and the author have become one. It's akin to befriending a like-minded soul. After a long time of reading, there are moments when you start confusing whether a comment is from the author or yourself. So, at some point, I developed the habit of marking my own thoughts with "<I>". It's a way to distinguish my thoughts. These <I>-marked notes later become the building blocks when I write.

When thorough reading became a habit, I paused at typographical errors. When I noticed a typo while reading, I instinctively corrected it.

There's no one-size-fits-all approach to reading. If you discover a reading approach that you'd like to emulate, feel free to adopt it. In matters of reading, a sense of freedom is desired. Books are lifelong companions and friends. Rather than imposing strict rules, let's embrace freedom and flexibility. Peace will naturally follow.

The path of a reader is a process of coloring our lives with beautiful autumn leaves. As autumn arrives, let's discover ourselves in tranquility, just as leaves reveal their beauty as they color themselves. No flower in the world has not bloomed. The only difference is whether or not that flower aligns with our desires.

Reading Books Begins with Leaders

When it comes to reading books at home, it starts with parents. In the workplace, it starts with leaders. A child who reads usually has parents who read, and in organizations that promote reading, their leaders read.

Books are the connecting umbilical cord between parents and children. They are the golden sustenance that nourishes leaders and organizations. Just as the nutrients from parents reach the child, the nourishment from leaders reaches the organization. The happiness of a home starts with parents, and the happiness of an organization starts with its leaders. The love from parents goes to the child, and the love from leaders goes to the organization. It's the natural flow from top to bottom.

A Leader: A Master of Thought, a Master of Listening

Reading is both relaxation and study. In the Joseon Dynasty, there was a system called 'Sagadokseoje,' a reading holiday for court scholars. This holiday was established in support of the leisure and research of the king's subjects. It was initiated by King Sejong the Great (1418-1450), the fourth monarch of the Joseon Dynasty.

King Sejong, who cherished and loved books from a young age, undoubtedly understood the sweetness of rest and study that books bring better than anyone else.

In the realm of learning, rest is necessary, and learning can occur during moments of rest. So, how about introducing the concept of a reading holiday to our companies?

Through the reading holiday, companies can explore current issues and seek solutions for the organization. How about starting with executives and leaders and gradually expanding the system over time? A leader is a thinker. More time is needed for thinking than for practical tasks.

Throughout the year, various moments should be reserved for thinking to clear paths. There is nothing quite like reading that enhances the ability to think.

If we look at the definition of thinking from the dictionary, it's described as the "act of observing and judging things." The foundation of the ability to observe things lies in reading. It allows for reading of gaining knowledge by the study of things. It means coming to attain knowledge by studying objects.

The reading holiday is not only a beautiful concept for companies but can also extend beyond national institutions to homes. The duration of the reading holiday could be adjusted considering the nature of each company and institution. Thinking and judgment abilities are crucial for leaders. Sound thinking leads to sound judgment, while shallow thinking leads to poor judgment.

Let's offer moments of contemplation as a gift to leaders. The value of contemplation becomes apparent through experience.

The 'reading holiday' is the greatest gift for leaders [Image source: Pixabay]

A leader is someone who listens. And books are the best tool for listening. This is because books are essentially the language of people.

In conversations, about 80% of the time is spent on listening.

Listening is ingrained in people who have a habit of reading. Through it, they have practiced listening. Only in the remaining 20% do they express their own thoughts. It's like the process of stirring rice when making porridge, which resembles listening. Pouring water in between is equivalent to speaking. The stirring process accounts for the majority of the process. The essence of language resides in listening. This is how one becomes a leader in communication.

King Sejong the Great was also a master of listening. He paid attention to scholarly discussions and the opinions of his ministers through discussion sessions. The annals of Sejong Chronicles record over two thousand sessions. Whether addressing his citizens or lower-ranking officials, King Sejong consistently maintained a posture of listening.

In the act of listening, the protagonist of the conversation is always the other party. Regardless of status, listening becomes natural when one treats the other as the protagonist. Remember that the protagonist is not the leader but always the other party. This applies from childhood to old age.

A Leader's Self-Esteem Determines the Organization

What is happiness? When parents are happy, their children are happy. When a leader is happy, the organization is happy. The source of happiness lies in self-esteem. In other words, it's love.

The degree to which we love ourselves determines the temperature of our love towards others. Those who know how to cherish and love themselves also hold others in high regard. Those who know they are flowers see others as flowers. It's because the mirror that reflects me also reflects the other person, just like how a small pupil holds the reflection of the other person's face.

If there are difficulties in managing an organization, one should first look inward. Is my self-esteem intact? If you dream of becoming a true leader, not just a manager, you must start by loving yourself. Before studying the organization, you need to study the art of self-love. If you closely examine problems, you'll find a deficiency in love in each one of them.

The root of all problems is a lack of love, and love should always begin with oneself.

Leaders with high self-esteem maintain an equal footing with others. Regardless of age or status, the level of one's eyes should be the same.

To see oneself clearly in the eyes of others, one's eye level needs to match. True communication is when the other person comfortably resides within our eyes, just like a camera capturing the other person.

When my mind is in the shape of a heart, the organization's shape is also of a heart
[Image source: Pixabay]

A leader is someone who refines their heart into a heart shape. Books can be helpful in this refinement. Characters in books have also left traces of refinement. Following these traces, while reading books, you'll find that your heart begins to dance.

A dancing heart carries smiles and love. It possesses the ability to illuminate wherever it rests.

The Journey That Follows
Reading is Writing

Writing is Love

To write is to love oneself. Furthermore, to write is to love the reader. Without self-love, you can't write. Without love for the reader, you can't write. Writing emerges from love. Think back to when we fell in love. We all become poets and writers. The reason is love.

Is there a greater power than love? The pinnacle of writing is cultivating the power of love. Allow me to share a piece of writing that expresses "love" beautifully, which I came across on social media.

The deeper meaning of "I LOVE YOU"

I: Inspire warmth

L: Listen to each other
O: Open your heart
V: Value your opinion
E: Express you trust

Y: Yield to good sense
O: Overlook mistakes
U: Understand differences

If our love towards readers is like so, how would our writing be? Let's replace the word 'you' with 'reader'. Writing is, in essence, an act of love. It's about giving love. If you have apprehensions about writing, think of it with ease. We are writing love. To write love, you must love yourself. Love is necessary to be able to give love.

Writers should fill their vessels of heart with love first [Image source: Pixabay]

The journey that follows reading is usually writing. Writing is the subject I am most interested in. It makes my heart leap every time and always comes across as something fresh. Among the lectures on writing, the most memorable statement I recall is: "The key to good writing is living life well. Writing comes from life," as said by author Kang Won Guk.

It's true. Writing is life. Writing emerges from life.

Our lives are all different. Because they are different, the same words can't be written. Just as peanuts from the same root appear different, even on the same topic, the content of writing varies. Therefore, even if the topic you want to write about already exists, there's no need to worry. It will be expressed in your own language, with your unique color, and the presence of similar topics might indicate an interested readership. So, let's slowly bring out our thoughts.

When writing doesn't flow easily, I seek the help of music. Music assists in refreshing our brains. Music affects writing. Upbeat and lively music brings forth cheerful writing. Emotional music results in soft and tender prose. Choosing music that suits the theme is also a method. If a piece of music makes you feel comfortable, it's suitable.

When writing, your mind should always be at ease. It's because writing holds the essence of the heart. Hastily written words will be read hastily, while peacefully composed text brings tranquility to the reader. A reader follows the author's breathing rhythm when reading.

The greatest gifts that writing offers are love and gratitude [Image source: Pixabay]

Three Important Habits for Writing

There are various elements to the habit of writing, but I'd like to highlight three.

The first is the habit of taking notes. Essential tools for writers are a small notebook and a pen. They should always be in your bag. Whenever a thought crosses your mind, jot it down immediately. The moment you think, "I'll remember this thought and write it down later," it tends to vanish. Letters have wings. A single line or even a single word will do. These sentences and words become the key to unlocking the essence of your writing. When you open the door with the key, the next sentences await you.

The habit of taking notes is important because even if you don't write right now, the material might be useful in the future. It's like gathering ingredients for cooking. Abundant ingredients enable a variety of dishes. The fruit of thoughts passing through your mind is more alive and fresher than any ingredient.

Now, let's move on to the two habits for smooth writing. There might be several, but among them, the two most crucial ones are reading out aloud and letting it sit.

Writing must be read aloud. When you read aloud, you'll stumble upon some blocks. You must remove those obstacles. Writing is like a forest of letters that readers walk through. If there are rocks or obstacles in the path, readers will stumble. You need to pick up the rocks to ensure a smooth walk through the forest of letters. The way to pick up those rocks is by repeatedly reading aloud.

During the revision process, it's crucial to print out your work and read it aloud repeatedly. With each repetition, your writing will become more polished.

Finally, there's letting it sit. In writing, it's akin to maturing kimchi. It requires giving it time to ferment. The reason well-aged kimchi tastes delicious is because it has undergone fermentation. It's about giving time to wait.

Once you've written a piece, it's best to let it sit for at least a week to ten days. Even if you felt there were no more sentences to improve, when you start looking at it again, new things emerge. It's almost as if your brain has had a rest and awakens once more. The process of tearing down a house made of letters also takes place after letting it sit. This is because it will be seen with fresh eyes.

After letting your writing sit and refining it, you'll get to taste well-matured kimchi. You will get to experience the deep taste of soybean stew made from soybean paste that has been slowly matured.

Above all, the secret to writing well is to refine our lives, frequently taste delicious dishes, and try our hand at cooking. It's about loving our lives, befriending great books, and composing our own pieces of writing.

Chapter 4

I PROPOSED – DREAMING OF A HAPPIER WORLD WITH BOOKS

(Three Proposals for a Happy Nation)

Books are a collection of all kinds of treasures

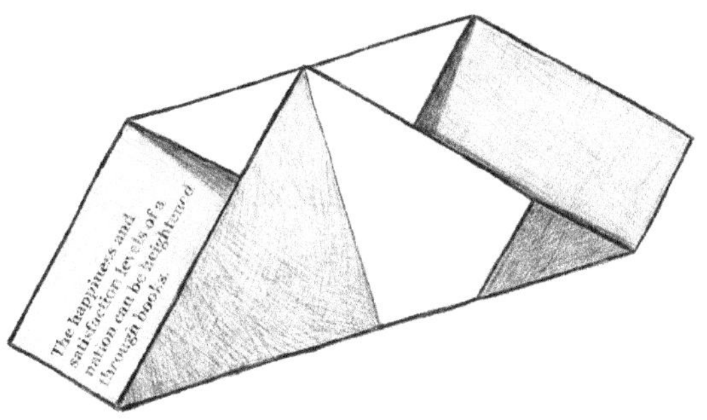

The Happiness and Satisfaction of a Nation Can Ben Heightened Through Books

Reading Begins at School and Work

The value of reading is too great to make it just an individual culture. Reading should occur in class and during office hours. Only then will reading become a habit. I would like to suggest 30 minutes before class starts and 30 minutes before work starts. At school, books are a treasure island. Books are a golden field at work. If you start your studies and work after peace of mind by reading a book, wouldn't you be more energized in your studies and work?

Studying and work are not proportional to time. The density of time is important. Reading is even more necessary to fill the remaining time in depth. This is because the 30 minutes in the morning are not wasted time. We may not be able to make all students good at studying, but wouldn't they at least learn how to find answers in books when they have a problem? What about when you graduate? You can give the reading habit as a gift. The same goes for work.

The best organization for a company is one that resembles nature. To resemble nature, employees must be happy above all else. The happiness of employees leads to the happiness of the company and ultimately to the happiness of society.

If you look closely at the trees on the mountain, you can see that there are many small trees next to the big trees. Trees communicate through their roots. Although we can't see it, we support and care for each other. Books are like this too. Knowledge in business is an idea. How about creating new ideas using the knowledge found in books? The ideas in the book are like a treasure island. What about wisdom? Wisdom in an organization means solving problems. More than tens of thousands of books are published every year. It is difficult to say that reading books makes you wise, but at least you can seek wisdom.

The best thing about corporate reading is that you can immediately apply it to your organization. Therefore, I want the 30 minutes after going to work to be free time for office workers' self-development, or at least for their bodies and minds.

For a company, one book is like planting a tree. Those trees will form a dense forest. The phytoncide of the tree becomes the scent of the tissue. If schools implement reading education and companies practice reading management, a reading nation will naturally be formed and the foundation of a happy nation will be laid.

Reading is something that brings light into the mind [Photo source: Pixabay]

How about talking about reading with a reading instructor at school or company about once a month and discussing any questions you have about reading books? I would be very happy if I gifted 30 minutes of morning reading as time to connect to the world of books.

I hope that reading education will fill the limitations that can't be filled through education at school and work. Reading and studying are not separate but embrace reading within studying. Just as a mountain embraces a lake, and the sky and earth embrace all things, studying is reading and reading is studying.

One of the greatest works of man is a book. Books are like treasures on Earth. Making a treasure and not using it is like planting an apple tree and not eating apple fruits. Sweet apples have love and happiness. We can bring love and happiness into our lives by consuming books. Books can make the world more beautiful and peaceful. Books are treasures that increase people's happiness and satisfaction.

Everyone knows that books are good. Everyone knows that apple fruits are delicious. When looking at the reasons for not being able to read in the National Reading Survey, the answer 'I don't have time' always ranks first. Twenty-four hours of modern people are always busy. I'm really short on time. But when you know the taste of books, you give yourself time.

Modern people need a break, and reading is the sweetest relaxation in the world. In order for reading to become a habit, you must first know the taste of reading. How can you gift the scarce time of modern people?

The average working hours in OECD countries is 1726 hours. The majority of countries exceed working hours. How about reflecting overtime working hours as a 30-minute morning reading culture? Reading should start first at school and at work.

If reading is done, reading will naturally become a habit.

A book is like planting an apple tree. The total number of people reading is the number of apple trees. The more apple trees you plant, the more sweet fruits you will eat. The more apple trees you plant, the more apples you can distribute to countries in need. Should the activity of reading be left only as a personal hobby?

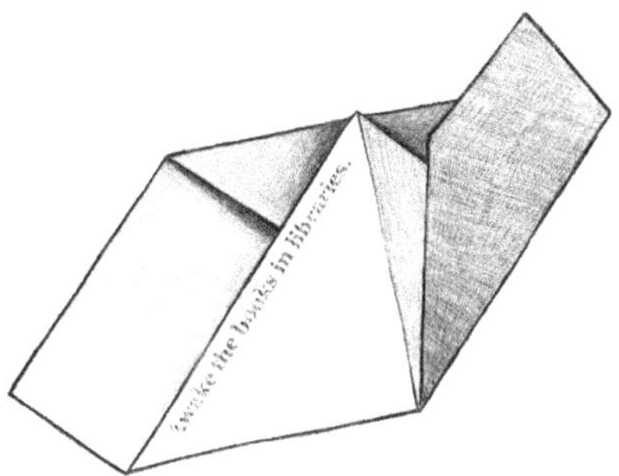

Awakening Books in the Library

How to Wake Up Library Books

Sometimes I've seen a mini library standing on the side of the road. When I came down from the hike one day, I was surprised to see a book on the side of the road. It was carefully designed to protect against rain. How about placing such mini libraries at bus stops in each country? You can come across books while waiting for the bus, local residents can look at books while walking, and sometimes even tourists can look at books. Furthermore, how about designating a mini library park and having a library within the park?

Hurray! I feel like traveling the world [Photo source: Pixabay]

I want to dance when I come to the park [Photo source: Pixabay]

In this way, you can see parents or caregivers reading books to their children, and you can also use it as a reading field trip to a daycare center or kindergarten. Sometimes, it is an opportunity to invite students outdoors to sail the ocean of books. Lovers can spread out a mat and read a book, and seniors can meet friends through a book.

A book is a mirror that reflects all things. Among all things, the first place that shines is ourselves. Looking at a book means looking at myself. Looking at me means looking at a book. The book is me, and I am the book.

After a lot of reading time, you will find out. The most beneficial thing about reading is 'the preciousness of life.' I am precious, the other person is precious, and everything I see is precious. The most fundamental value among all preciousness is to know your own preciousness first. If you know your own worth first, you will be able to see the other person's worth.

That preciousness is 'love'. Looking at the etymology of love, it comes from the Latin word 'Lubere', which means 'to rejoice'. The benefit of reading is knowing love and enjoying the joy of the present. Don't put off today's joy until tomorrow.

Today's joy belongs to today. Tomorrow's joy belongs to tomorrow. You must fully enjoy the joy of today. The most important day in the world is today. Knowing the joy of today and making us aware of the importance of today is the power of books.

Above all, you will experience the value of yourself. It makes me feel grateful for everything.

The First Step Towards a Happy Nation is 30-minute Morning Reading Culture

What if we brought books from the library into school classrooms or businesses to wake up the books in the library? How about borrowing books from the school library for classroom books, and how about borrowing books from the local library for corporate books? Library books can be loaned not only to individuals but also to groups, so why not take advantage of the library's loan system for each company? It is quite difficult for busy office workers to borrow books from the library, so as part of revitalizing books in libraries, I propose using corporate group loans.

Activating corporate group lending can open up opportunities for reading to employees. Since you can't underline a book, important parts will naturally be written down in your notebook. You can apply the important content written in your notes directly to your organization, or you can try to incorporate them into small habits in your life. If books become part of a company's organizational culture, it will see remarkable growth.

If you look closely at great companies and great talent, there are always books there.

30 minutes in the morning is just for myself [Photo source: Pixabay]

I hope all schools and workplaces consider the 30-minute morning reading culture.

School reading refers to the period from daycare to graduate school. The workplace refers to the place of employment in all employment relationships.

No matter how much money you have, time is limited. Isn't one of the most precious things in the world giving time as a gift to someone else? The first step to a happy society is giving time to love myself. People who can communicate well with themselves can enjoy conversations with anyone.

Especially if there are difficulties in the school and organizational culture, it is even more important to gift 'me' time to students and employees. If faculty, CEOs, and those who work in government agencies also have 'me time' on a regular basis, our society will become gentler. It's natural for the people's happiness and satisfaction index to increase.

A Day for Gifting Books, Like Valentine's Day

There's Valentine's Day for loved ones, and there's White Day. How about one day of the year as book gift day? And on that day, people give books as gifts to their loved ones. Designating a 'Book Gift Day' will greatly increase the number of people reading books.

The new year is a happy day for everyone. A year has passed, and we prepare for a new day with a new mind. We welcome the new day with a new heart and the light of the rising red sun. As we welcome the new year, what if the country started gifting books?

In Korea, when a child is born, the government gives a first book gift. What if we expanded that event to the entire life, not just the first year? Of course, you'll need to consider your budget, but I would like to suggest this to many countries around the world. You should not skimp on the cost of books, as the value of a book is like many stars.

Once the government opens a waterway, the next steps become natural. Once you get to know the taste of a book, you will naturally be curious about the next taste. Through books, families can communicate more, and lovers can understand each other better. A book will solve many problems. It's truly a pity that the greatest treasure on earth is not actively used. Anyone who loves books knows that books are treasures. People who read books should be the public, not the minority.

The culture of reading books must go beyond the current generation and become a national culture in the next generation and the generations after that. The starting point is the current generation. There is no era in which reading is not necessary, but reading will be a great help in these difficult times.

Books are a window to see the beauty of Mother Nature [Photo source: Pixabay]

In the case of global companies, there was a culture of giving books as gifts to employees. I was truly happy and surprised to see that. I, too, was happy to recommend a valuable book that I would like to share. The first step to becoming a key talent is to give a book as a gift, and the second is to give the gift of time to read a book.

Companies expect their employees to do their jobs well and achieve more results. That powerful tool is a book. Books are gifts for both companies and individuals. This is because numerous ideas and products of human wisdom are melted there. The type written in the book is gold. I hope that the culture of giving books as gifts to valuable employees will gradually spread to small and medium-sized companies, starting with large global companies.

So which book should you choose?

Bookstores and libraries are places full of treasures. However, when you actually try to choose a book, it can be difficult to know which. More than tens of thousands of books are published every year, and books are divided into only major categories, so readers may have difficulty making a choice. How about breaking down the categories to find out who should read this book, whether they are beginner or intermediate readers, and what kind of help it can provide? How about making improvements after identifying the needs of readers?

People who are going to read the book obviously want to find the nutrients they need right now. Choosing a book will be easier if you provide hints to help you find that nutrient.

One more thing I would like to suggest is that places that recommend books, such as schools and organizations, combat scatteredness. There will be clear reasons for the recommendation. How about gathering recommended books in one place? Through this, readers can search for recommended books at libraries or bookstores nationwide and find the books they need at any time.

To add to that idea, we show readers books on the nutrients they need right now through a simple question check in a quiz format? It's like when a person enters a clothing store, the clerk asks the customer what style they want and recommends clothes. Of course, you should not forget that recommended books are just recommendations, and that you are the owner of the book.

The purpose of recommended books is to serve an auxiliary role to help. Also, every author of a book has a central message they want to convey to their readers. How about telling that message directly in the author's voice?

It's good to listen to a sample of a book, and it's also good to include a message to convey to readers. The author's voice will play a big role in the reader's understanding of the book and the bond with the reader.

I hope that the role of online bookstores will increase in importance as a bridge that firmly connects authors and readers. The role of online bookstores is very important in helping readers choose books and become readers. It would also be nice to have the ability to follow authors directly, as in the case of Amazon.com. If improvements are made by focusing on the role of bridge between authors and readers, there will be more readers who love books.

Also, why not set up a children's space in your bookstore and offer free samples of children's books? I hope to see more books as samples in a larger space. There may be many reasons, but I always want there to be enough space for children. This is because the future talent is children. Bookstores play a very important role in making reading a habit for children.

I hope that the culture of giving books as gifts will be realized naturally. To that end, a service that packages books will also be helpful. Books are love and gratitude. It's one of the best products and blessings that humans leave behind on Earth.

Chapter 5

I COMPOSED – THE DISCOVERY OF READING

The magic of life begins when you walk through a
book garden and follow your inner passion

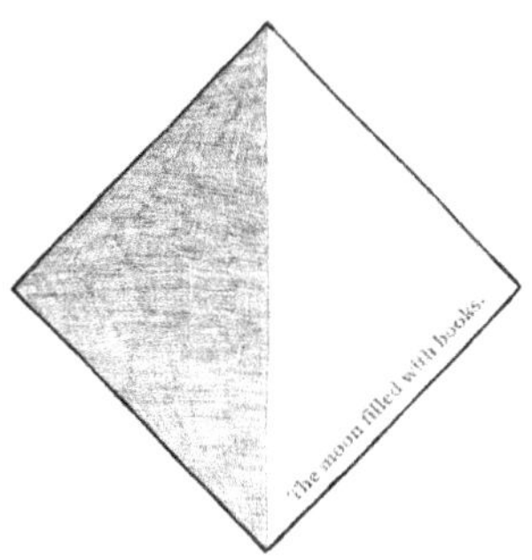

The Moon Filled with Books

All things in high places have light.
Then why does the moon hang in the sky?
Do not question.
See the moon's heart,
round and round.

Beautiful heart of the moon,
the sun gifted a mirror of light.

The moon that loves books is rather shy,
appearing slender as a crescent moon,
gaining a bit more courage,
revealing itself coyly as a half-moon.

Yet,
the moon is not always just shy.

Sometimes it goes, "Ta-da!"
Showing its whole self.
Why, we've seen the full moon.
It's shy, but not always hiding away.

With the force of grandeur, it brightens the pitch-black night.
Even the passing snail must be amazed.

At times it even performs on stage,
a rainbow performance,
a collection of moonbeams.

The moon filled with books;
its lovely heart
cannot be concealed.

The moon filled with books;
its golden light
brightens the world.

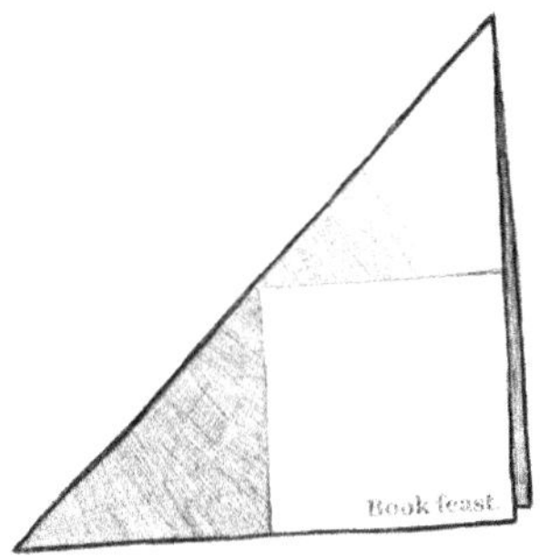

Book Feast

Within books, all sorts of dishes can be found.
The matured and rich flavors are exquisite.

There's joy in choosing what to eat according to your taste.
So don't grimace; just read a book.

Worry not what you're going to eat today.

For when you visit a bookstore, various dishes of the world await.
Worry not if you have no money to spend.
In the library, various dishes await.

My food, my family's food.
Let's choose together
a bountiful feast.
Let's indulge.

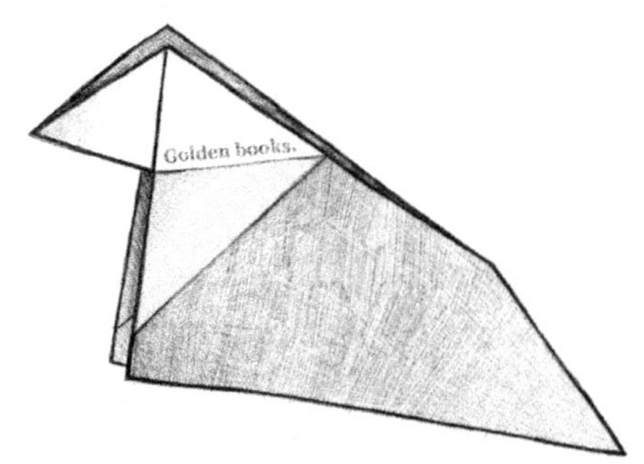

Golden Book

Searching in mines to extract gold
for no reason at all.
Polished over and over again,
letters are engraved in gold.

Take as much as you need.
Add them to your life.

Take as much as you need.
Fill your belly.

Here's gold.
There's gold, too.
Gold is everywhere.

A place full of treasure
are bookstores and libraries.

Awakening Books in the Library

In the library, there sleeps tens of thousands of books.
Resting for too long is harmful to their health.

Awaiting a breeze and the touch of human hands.
Yet for decades, they have slept.
No one has awakened them.

They wait with reddened eyes once again today.
Still, only tranquility flows.

When will they be awakened?
Only the sound of a sigh can be heard today again.

How do we awaken the books in the library?
Borrowing comes first.

To every workplace across the world,
they must be set free.

Only when touched by working hands
are the books brought to life.

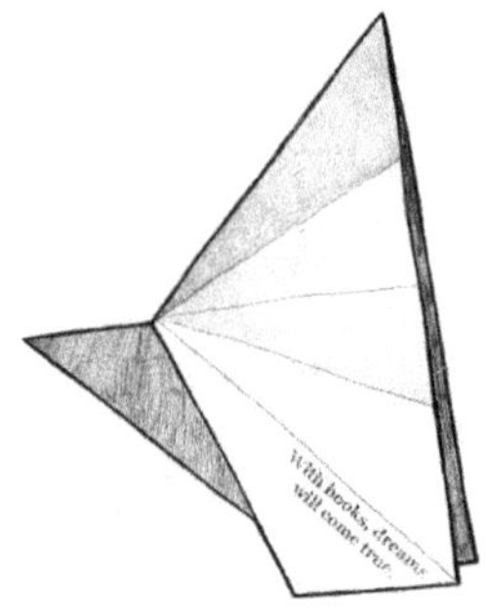

With Books,
Dreams Will Come True

Dreamers
under the blue sky,
gaze at the stars.

Even when the dazzling sun blinds them,
even when the feathery clouds obscure the view,
dreamers still know
the stars are there.

Though clouds weep sadly,
turning into raindrops,
dreamers still know
the stars are there.

The reason they know the stars are there
is that they shot up the stars themselves.

When the time comes,
their light will shine
when accompanied by books.

PEOPLE I MET AT MOONLIGHT LIBRARY

Interviews with Distinguished Authors

(Source: Korea Institute of Human Resources Development in Science and Technology (KIRD) K-CLUB Interviews)

Meeting great people is like visiting the library of their soul

Meeting Professor Kim Beomjun, a Philosopher of Science, Sungkyunkwan University

I had the chance to meet Professor Kim Beomjun, a philosopher of science. He recently published *I Asked Newton Who I Am*. Reading this book, I became curious about the source of the strength to understand and realize one's existence through the journey of physics. As I talked with Professor Kim, it seemed that this strength emerged from his beautiful inner self. Just like Professor Kim mentioned, in comparison to the vast universe, we are tiny and insignificant like dust, making us even more precious. Through this mini-interview, which reflects Professor Kim's life and philosophy, we will get to discover a better version of ourselves.

Kim Beomjun, Professor of Physics at Sungkyunkwan University

Could you introduce yourself?

I am Kim Beomjun, teaching students at the Department of Physics at Sungkyunkwan University. My specialized field in physics is statistical physics. Statistical physics is one of the traditional majors in physics. The primary focus of statistical physicists is to study macroscopic phenomena in physical systems composed of many particles.

In the past, research mainly revolved around systems with many particles, but since the year 2000, the scope of research has started to expand. These days, beyond physical systems composed of many particles, research is being conducted on economic phenomena involving societies or economic entities composed of many individuals. This research is carried out in a manner similar to studying physical systems. I also focus on research in that field.

Also, I have compiled the results of my research into several books. I have a keen interest in diffusing physics to the public through book publications and in connecting with and communicating with people who are not physics majors.

It seems you've chosen a job that you enjoy. I heard that you dreamed of becoming a scientist influenced by Carl Sagan's book, *Cosmos*, when you were in 7th grade. I'm curious about how you turned that childhood dream into reality.

I consider myself a happy scientist because I've fulfilled the aspiration I had when I was young. As such, I don't think there are any particular secrets or tricks to share.

Looking back on my experiences, I believe that interest, curiosity, and excitement were the most important things. Both studying and conducting research during graduate school were interesting to me. As I continued to live with excitement, I ended up living the life of a scientist that I had wished for when I was young.

Although everyone's path may differ a bit, I had significantly different grades in subjects I liked compared to the ones I didn't during university. When you see this, it seems that when you enjoy something, you naturally put more effort into it. As you keep making efforts, you get better at it, and as you get better, you enjoy it more. So, in order to achieve dreams, I believe it's most important to maintain and not lose interest.

What advice would you give to students who are currently pondering their career paths?

I'm not sure if I'm qualified to provide this kind of advice, as I do not have a lot of life experiences. However, I've observed something through the graduate students who have graduated from my research group and others. I hope they don't feel afraid of trying what they are drawn to or what they want to do.

For instance, among my younger friends, there are cases where they want to change their career or environment to the field they desire, but they can't make a decision due to practical concerns. They worry that if they change their job, they would only get to see their spouses on weekends due to working locations, or they'll have to move to a smaller house that is less comfortable than their current home. Looking back, I realize that these practical worries are often insignificant in the grand scheme of things. I hope they don't give up on their dreams and desires too easily due to these practical concerns.

Just give it a try.

You mentioned in your book, meeting a person on this planet, as we coexist in the same era on Earth, is a result of an astonishing astronomical coincidence. Every encounter is a precious astronomical event. People often struggle with relationships within this small planet. Can you share your unique advice or insights into human relationships?

Each of us is a precious encounter to another [Image source: Pixabay]

I wrote that phrase thinking, "How precious is it for two people to meet within this vast universe?" I don't have any special secrets about human relationships. Like others, I also find human relationships challenging. So, I'm not sure if there's any unique advice on human relationships as a physicist.

However, as I've written in that phrase, aren't we all very precious existences? Whether it's a bad encounter or a good one, I believe that everything is precious. While it's hard to call it a secret, when I encounter someone I don't particularly like, I try to see the finer details when they are nearby.

Back in middle and high school, there were classmates who were not kind to others. Once, I closely observed the bag one of those classmates was carrying, and I noticed a stitching mark where their mother had repaired a tear. That made me think, "Ah, this fella may be a little mean to others, but he must be of a precious presence at home to his mother." After that, he didn't seem as mean as he did before.

Even now, when I'm disappointed in people's relationships, I try to see their finer details. When you look at their small and ordinary sides, you realize they are just like you.

"We are stardust. But a very special form of stardust, self-aware." That's quite an impressive phrase. Who do you think you are in this vast universe? And what kind of mindset should people have within this universe?

Humans are like specks of dust, making their existence even more precious
[Image source: Pixabay]

The existence of a star refers to a humble existence, much like a tiny speck.

As insignificant as dust, yet a unique form of existence as humans. I've pondered about that. So, in this universe, what kind of mindset should we have? When I think of words like 'universe' and 'humans', it leads me to believe that each individual human is so small, like a tiny speck, that they become an even more precious existence. For example, we find spring flowers beautiful, but wouldn't we not find them as precious if those flowers covered the entire world and bloomed all year round? Thinking in this way, humans could be seen as even more precious due to their small and insignificant nature.

Could you share your special self-care and mental health management methods?

Just like any other human being, I live my life by experiencing both wounds and pleasures. My honest belief is that when you reach around the age of forty, you don't change much. It's not possible to try to change someone who doesn't match your ideal image of them. The best way to manage your mental state is to acknowledge that both you and the other person are different entities.

Reflecting on this, I realized I'm the same. Simply listening to someone doesn't change me easily. Others would be the same. So, don't try too hard to change them. Remember that you are different, not wrong. Recognizing this and making efforts based on it is crucial.

You mentioned, "Science is ultimately about creating maps." You also emphasized that it's important for researchers to acknowledge that maps can differ and to respect each other's maps. Can you offer advice on the desirable roles and attitudes for students who are embarking on the path of researchers?

Science is the act of creating maps [Image source: Pixabay]

A true scientist is a person who respects [Image source: Pixabay]

If science involves creating maps in different areas of study, the map of a physicist and a chemist, would be different. However, I realized that it would not be fair to say that the physicist's map is superior when it comes to understanding the world of a chemist. So, respecting each other's maps, not thinking that your map is superior to others, is necessary. There's no reason to think it's superior.

Many people, after immersing themselves in a particular field for a long time, might misunderstand and think that research in other fields is somewhat inferior to their own. I want to say that this is not the case. I hope more people understand that there isn't only one.

These days, interdisciplinary research is a common topic. Having your own perspective while respecting the perspectives of researchers from other fields is a desirable form of interdisciplinary research.

No matter how hard I try, it's difficult for me to see the world through the eyes of a sociologist. Similarly, viewing the world through the eyes of a physicist is just as valuable as viewing it through the eyes of a sociologist. Therefore, a desirable role and attitude for a researcher would be respect.

Lastly, could you share a message of encouragement for science and technology professionals who are striving for career development?

Fill with reading, experiences, and passion [Image source: Pixabay]

The future of all of us is uncertain. I hope you see your career development as preparation for the uncertainties you will encounter. Preparing for uncertainties should be both broad and deep. Alongside a wide-ranging knowledge of various fields, you should possess in-depth knowledge of the field you hope to be engaged in the future. I hope you equip yourself with a wide range of reading, diverse experiences, and an unceasing passion for your field. I'm rooting for all of you!

Source: Korea Institute of Human Resources Development in Science and Technology
(KIRD) K-CLUB Interviews

Interview book: Written by Kim Beomjun, published by 21st Century Books,
I Asked Newton Who I Am

Meeting Professor Hwang Nongmun, Scholar of Happiness in the Field of Education

I read the book *Slow Thinking* by Professor Hwang Nongmun, who is already well-known as an expert in immersion. It felt like encountering an ancient sage. I began to think of Professor Hwang as a true scholar of education. Through our interview, I realized that the professor is a 'happiness scholar in the scientific world. Professor Hwang shared, "Value the unique opportunity of your one and only life, and live a life where you can fully unleash your abilities." In this mini-interview, which encapsulates Professor Hwang's life and philosophy, we can gather tips on how to love our jobs and how to live a regret-free life. Moreover, in our hearts, words like courage and challenge will gradually find their place.

Professor Hwang Nongmun, Department of Materials Science and Engineering at Seoul National University

Could you introduce yourself?

In February 2003, I became a professor in the Department of Materials Science and Engineering at Seoul National University and have been studying with my students since then. I have been working on establishing problem-solving methods of thinking that analyze the thought processes of geniuses like Newton and Einstein, aiming to maximize brain utilization.

I also actively contribute as a troubleshooter for quality issues in industrial production processes using this thinking approach. Furthermore, I apply these thinking techniques to creative corporate management, and I also engage as a promoter of thinking in education, emphasizing learning and fostering creativity.

You mentioned, "The secret of happiness is not doing what I like but liking what I do." What are some ways to enjoy what we do?

This idea is similar to what was said by J.M. Barrie, the author of *Peter Pan* and closely aligns with the insights I gained through immersion. Living life, you cannot escape 'work,' and work consumes the most time in one's lifetime. Realistically speaking, pursuing happiness while doing what you love doesn't result in much attainable happiness. Life might even become more challenging at times. However, if you like what you do or learn to like your work, the amount of happiness you can attain increases, and the performance of your work also improves.

According to neuroscience, happiness is related to the secretion of positive brain chemicals. Immersion triggers the secretion of positive chemicals. When you immerse yourself in the work you need to carry out, happy hormones are released, making you like the task and experience a sense of happiness. It's easier to immerse yourself in things you like, but it's often difficult to do so for your job or work you need to carry out.

In such cases, I practice 'deliberate immersion'. The effectiveness of deliberate immersion has been verified in many cases. Even in tasks you don't enjoy, raising your level of deliberate immersion can make the task manageable and eventually enjoyable. It can even become something you like.

The secret of happiness is liking what I do [Image source: Pixabay]

You mentioned, "What we fear is not life itself but regretting that we let our one and only life pass." How do you define life? What kind of life should we pursue?

My interest in living a life without regret dates back to my middle and high school years. Back then, I needed to study hard to get into a prestigious school, but instead of giving my best effort, I wasted most of my time, repeating days of failure. As these days repeated, the pain of regret intensified, and I eventually realized that the most feared thing in the world is regret.

Then one day, I thought, "After a failed day, there's another day, and after a failed year, there's another year, but after a failed life, there's no other life." At that moment, I realized that if I were to regret at the end of my life that I lived it poorly, there would be no way to console myself. This led me to consider how to live in such a way that there would be no regrets on the last day of my life. This question has since become the focus of my life.

Until then, I hadn't found an answer to this question because I didn't truly understand the meaning of 'regret'. Regret isn't about what to do or what profession to have. It's about how to live. It's about the process rather than the result. If I make full use of all my abilities, regardless of the profession or task, I won't have regrets when I die. Our current existence offers the only opportunity to experience this world. So, I want to convey the message of valuing this unique opportunity and living a life where you can fully spread the wings of your abilities.

Treasure the opportunity of your one and only life [Image source: Pixabay]

You mentioned that, "The most outstanding ideas exist in sleep and dreams." Could you please provide tips for obtaining outstanding ideas?

When our level of immersion is low, no matter how much we think, remarkable ideas don't come to mind. Extraordinary ideas tend to surface with a higher frequency when in a state of immersion. The principle behind the emergence of ideas that I've come to understand is as follows. Our brain not only stores memories but also retrieves them. The emergence of ideas means that long-term memories related to the problems we're trying to solve are being retrieved through consciousness. To think well is essentially "a state in which the brain is adept at retrieving long-term memories." The brain is more adept at retrieving long-term memories during sleep than during periods of wakefulness. This is because during sleep, a neurotransmitter called acetylcholine, which is involved in memory retrieval, is secreted in larger amounts, and the prefrontal cortex becomes inactive, allowing long-term memories buried deep within the subconscious to be more easily retrieved.

Therefore, in order to obtain exceptional ideas, you should utilize sleep. If you train yourself to be in a state of thinking about a given problem even while you're asleep, you can employ creativity even during sleep. In other words, you need to create a state of 'lucid sleep'. To reach this state, you need to continuously think about the problem for several days without rest. By doing this, you can experience a flood of creative ideas.

You mentioned that, "While artificial intelligence may replace human jobs, the value of exceptional talents with creativity will, if anything, increase infinitely in the era of the Fourth Industrial Revolution." What are some methods to foster creativity?

From history, we can learn a typical method for fostering creativity, and I believe that is the educational methods of Socrates and Confucius. Both Socrates and Confucius guided their disciples to think and acquire knowledge for themselves through questioning, rather than directly transmitting knowledge or wisdom. They prompted their students to arrive at realizations through additional questions even when they answered incorrectly, allowing them to learn through introspection. Many people talk about the importance of creative education, yet often don't know how to execute it.

In my view, creative education can be summed up as 'brain development education'. In traditional rote education, acquiring knowledge was set as the primary goal, but in creative education, the first goal is to develop the brain, with knowledge acquisition being secondary.

Hence, even when faced with unknown problems, instead of being taught how to solve problems, I recommend learning by pondering and finding answers on your own, even if it takes time. Instead of solving numerous problems within a given time simultaneously, I recommend a study method where you take your time to solve one problem, reflecting upon it. This method encourages you to think critically and not give up, helping you to develop your brain. Through this approach, you can enhance your ability to solve problems creatively, regardless of the nature of the problem. Furthermore, while solving unknown problems on your own, you'll automatically acquire a deep understanding of the knowledge involved.

Could you please share your unique reading method and some books that have left a strong impression on you?

Make reading a habit of life [Image source: Pixabay]

I approach reading with careful selection and focus. I choose books thoughtfully and read them repeatedly. So, when I read, I underline the important parts that I want to read again. If there are noteworthy ideas, I jot them down in a separate notebook along with my thoughts. If there are concepts I don't quite grasp, I use question marks. Given that I underline, take notes, and use question marks, I rarely borrow books from the library since I need to interact with the text.

Among the relatively recent books I've read, some that left a deep impression include *Synaptic Self* by Joseph LeDoux, *Why God Won't Go Away* by Andrew Newberg, *Talent is Overrated* by Geoff Colvin, *Israel's Edge* by Jason Gewirtz, *Toegye and Japanese Learning* by Yoshio Abe, and *Mind Training of Joseon Scholars, Sitting Still* by Choi Seokgi.

"To truly love something, you must undergo rigorous training, shed many tears, and delve into deep wanderings. Only by devoting yourself completely to that endeavor can you genuinely come to love it." This is quite impactful. Could you please provide methods for overcoming slumps and ways to love one's work, particularly for researchers?

When I entered a science and engineering university, I had to choose my major by the end of the first year. Without much thought, I chose metallurgical engineering. However, as I started taking major courses, I realized that metallurgical engineering was not a suitable field for my aptitude. A major is something you engage with for a lifetime, and the thought of living with something so uninteresting depressed me. Yet, during my graduate studies, I found research activities that required me to think deeply fascinating. But my chosen field of study primarily had pragmatic value as a means of livelihood. Yet, with full dedication and immersion, it evolved into a truly interesting field.

Over an extended period, through complete immersion in your research like your life depends on it, various transformations occur. When the work you do feels more precious than your own life, a sense of vocation begins to emerge. Once you develop a sense of vocation, you feel profoundly grateful and happy for the opportunity to perform that work.

Even if a research topic changed, I have repeatedly experienced that the same emotions arise if I approach it with complete dedication and immersion. This led me to believe that I am the one responsible for creating the work I genuinely love. Thus, if someone doesn't find much significance in their work, I would recommend immersing themselves in it as if their life depended on it for about a month. This will likely lead them to perceive their work as not only interesting and meaningful but even noble.

During a slump, the best option is to love work [Image source: Pixabay]

You said, "The secret of those who climb the uphill of life and stand on the summit are those who find joy in facing challenges without hesitation and in the processes rather than results." You described those with the ability to think as slow thinkers. Could you please share a message of encouragement with science and technology professionals who aspire to become slow thinkers?

Live a life without regrets [Image source: Pixabay]

Jon Gordon, a motivational expert, says the following.

"Everything worthwhile in life is uphill. What's valuable in life, what you hope for and want to achieve, what you want to enjoy, it's all uphill. The problem is, most people have uphill dreams, but downhill habits."

To solve life's equation or tackle life's challenges, we must learn to go uphill against our instinctual tendency that leans toward the downhill path. What I've realized about climbing the uphill of life is experiencing the feeling of "it felt so good to reach the summit." This allows our brain to replace the painful and negative memories of the uphill process with positive memories of the summit, motivating us to take on the uphill challenge again.

Easy challenges pose no problem. But sometimes challenges seem too difficult or even impossible. What do you do then? Instead of fixating on the outcome, focus on the process with a dedicated mindset. For instance, when I took on a challenge in the field of materials that had gone unsolved for over fifty years, my mindset was as follows.

"This problem may never be solved in my lifetime. I might only be able to solve about 40% of it before my life ends. But it doesn't matter. The remaining 60% I can't solve could be solved by someone else. The fact is, I will do my best. I will ignite my life without resting a second." By placing meaning in the process rather than obsessing over the outcome, you can challenge even seemingly impossible tasks. This is achievable by everyone. I support your life journey.

Source: Korea Institute of Human Resources Development in Science and Technology (KIRD) K-CLUB Interviews

Interview book: "Slowing Thinking" by Hwang Nongmun, Wisdom House

Meeting Professor Yoo Yeongman, a Knowledge Ecologist in the Field of Education

I had the opportunity to meet Professor Yoo Yeongman, a knowledge ecologist in the field of education. Reading his recent book, *Writing a Book Requires Great Effort*, I was able to reflect more deeply on the essence of writing books. His secret to writing ninety-odd volumes of work and translations lies in his willingness to face challenges and practical life approach. The book contained wisdom engraved through practical experience. We will explore the life and philosophy of Professor Yoo through a mini-interview on writing books. Let's delve into his precious message, "Anyone can write a book."

Professor Yoo Yeongman, Department of Educational Technology, Hanyang University

Could you introduce yourself?

I consider myself more of a knowledge ecologist than a university professor. I study how organisms in nature live, their principles, and methods of living. Extracting the principles of how they live and using them to change people's thoughts and transform organizations is the interdisciplinary field of knowledge ecology.

For a long time, the answers we seek have been in nature. Nature is not something to be protected; it's a subject we should constantly learn from and become familiar with. Humans should play with nature from a young age, but as time goes on, we often distance ourselves from nature and end up studying only at our desks.

I'm not only a professor, but also a writer and a lecturer. I aim to capture experiences, observations, and realizations in my books. Through these books, I deliver lectures and pour out joy and passion to change people through education.

You said, "A resonating piece of writing can only be authored by someone who has experienced resonance. Only those who have been shaken can write something that shakes the world." What you said is quite impressive. What has been the most significant event in your life when you experienced resonance?

I believe our lives are a collective work of thoughts. Within every event lies an untellable story, and within that grows contemplation. When we experience thinking, thoughts and contemplations meet, and thinking changes. Although we might experience thoughts passively, passive thinking generates active thinking. There have been many events, but the most significant turning point that led me here was encountering a particular book while I was welding at the Pyeongtaek Thermal Power Plant.

It was a book about someone's experience in passing the bar exam. It planted a misguided dream in me that I, too, should study for the bar exam. Books can revolutionize people. Like how a cucumber turns into a pickle but can never become a cucumber again, books cause irreversible transformations. That book served as the turning point that led me here, and the event of deciding to quit studying for the bar exam, whether to study further or burn books overnight, was also significant. I gave up on the bar exam because I thought if I continued with uninteresting studies, my life would be uninteresting.

While there have been numerous events and incidents, such events generate new contemplations in me and become material for my books. Another significant event was falling deeply into reading books after that incident.

You wrote, "Writing is a collaborative work stains and patterns left behind from 'living,' 'reading,' and 'creating'." What advice do you have for science and technology professionals who dream of writing books about the kind of mindset required to write?

Unless our lives change, our writing won't change either. Writing is a work of life itself. It's also an asset created by life. Many people constantly try to learn the technique of writing, but before learning that, they need to create a topic. That topic is simply living a life different from before. People who don't live a life different from before can't write something different from before. Trying to write differently while living the same life is not right.

Another aspect is that if you write based solely on your own life, you might fall into the fallacy of sitting in a well and looking up at the sky. You need to meet people who live in different worlds from you. You can meet them directly or indirectly. Indirect encounters involve reading their books. So, both living and reading are necessary to generate new writing that has the two combined.

The reason for distinguishing between writing and book writing is that being good at writing doesn't necessarily mean you can write a book. Writing is a short-distance race, but writing a book is a long-distance marathon. Only when you're able to write, can you prepare to write a book. So, even science and technology professionals need to write if they want to create literature. Improvement in writing only happens through writing itself. If you stare at a blank page all day without writing, your mind also becomes blank. But once you write a single line, interestingly, that sentence brings another sentence. And it continues. So, you must start writing.

** Sitting in a well and looking at the sky: This phrase indicates one having a very narrow perspective; similar to the saying 'a big fish in a small pond'*

** Source: Naver Encyclopedia*

The source of writing is finding that 1cm difference from yesterday [Image source: Pixabay]

You wrote, "Everyone has one word that they hold in their hearts. It's a word like a tow truck that guides one's life which one would be willing to trade it with one's life." You mentioned that your last word is 'challenge'. What kind of challenge are you currently dreaming of? And what challenges are needed for those who want to write, in your opinion?

You can learn knowledge at your desk, but wisdom can only be learned through practice. That's why it's called practical wisdom and experiential wisdom. I prefer those with innate wisdom over knowledgeable individuals, and instinctive individuals over those with innate wisdom.

Starting from the second semester of this year, I'll be taking a sabbatical for a year. I plan to become a cab driver. I believe it's the best way to engage with people who live challenging lives in a confined space. Hence, I need to acquire a cab driver's license. I also plan to go on a cross-country trip on a bicycle.

When the COVID-19 situation gets better, another dream of mine is hiking. I'm planning to climb Mount Elbrus (5,642m), known as the highest peak in Europe. Taking up a challenge that can help me change once a year can bring much joy and excitement as I prepare for it.

For those who want to write, you need unique material. Without unique challenges, unique writing won't emerge. A challenge doesn't need to be grand like crossing the Sahara Desert, but living a life different from yesterday is itself a challenge. For example, if you always eat with colleagues, try having a meal with someone new. This can bring fresh inspiration. It's about trying different methods than what you used before. If you usually take the bus and subway to work, try walking half the way or cycling. Every different attempt is a challenge. This way, you gain new insights and discover new methods. Methods don't just come from sitting and thinking. You need to experience to come up with new methods. If you're into reading, don't just stick to the same type of books. Instead, read books from entirely different fields. All of this is a new intellectual challenge.

You said, "Reading doesn't end when you turn the last page of a book. True reading begins from that moment." Could you share your unique method of reading?

There may be various methods of reading, but I believe in thorough reading. For example, if you read Nietzsche's *Thus Spoke Zarathustra* in a rush, it would be hard to understand. Instead of reading many different books, read the same one multiple times.

After reading it once and then reading it again, you might discover different meanings. Since the author's life is different from yours, you might not understand it on the first read. But instead of putting it away as incomprehensible, it's important to chew on it, read it again, and go through that process. And after you finish reading, you might not remember what you've read. That's why I have my secret quote notebook. Since our hands are like a second brain, I jot down notes by hand. I inscribe each sentence as if carving it in with a hot iron. While writing by hand, I can reconsider the author's meaning and ponder it once more. I mark the needed parts using sticky notes for reference. I then type those marked parts on A4 paper to create my reading notes.

When writing a book, I appropriately quote these sentences and back up my arguments. I don't just read books; I read while writing, and I write while reading. My reading and writing are so intertwined that they can't be easily separated. When writing a book on a certain topic, I both read and write about it simultaneously.

Reading is the act of making the treasures within books our own [Image source: Pixabay]

You said, "Writing is a bojagi (a traditional Korean wrapping cloth). A bojagi is completely orientated around the other, not itself. Unlike a bag, it doesn't place itself at the center but puts the other at the center, humbling and embracing the other, symbolizing the virtue." Why is the reader essential in writing, in your view?

The difference between writing and a book is that writing doesn't have to be read by someone, but a book must be read by readers. If readers don't read it, it negatively impacts the publisher. Therefore, always remember that a book must be read by readers and consider readers' perspectives to make sure they can resonate with it.

You must constantly think about readers, understanding their pain points, what they're curious about, and what they desire. You need to frequently tap into readers' perspectives. Always think about how to establish a connection with readers, what language, and empathetic codes to use.

You mentioned, "Writing should be done whenever you have thoughts and whenever inspiration strikes. That's the path for a writer who infuses his or her life into writing. Treat it like breathing." Why is having habits important in our lives?

If you write sporadically, the context and flow of your writing can be disjointed. You might even forget what you wrote. You can only develop the muscles for writing through periodically repeating concentrated writing sessions over a certain period. Establishing the continuity of context and coherence in your writing requires dedicating an hour or two to practice the process of stringing together your thoughts cohesively on a single topic.

First of all, regularity is important. Ideally, you should write daily, but if that's too challenging, aim to write habitually for at least once every two days, during a set time, writing a set amount. It's ideal when you feel the desire to write as if you're hungry or thirsty. Once you start writing and editing, you'll end up with a form of writing that's completely different from your first draft. The importance of habits lies in how these points accumulate, coming together to create something.

Bread needs to mature to become soft. Writing, too, is like bread [Image source: Pixabay]

You said, "Just like how cucumbers become pickles and cabbage turns into kimchi through the process of fermentation and maturation, writing also matures as the pieces of writing that encapsulate the author's life accumulate over time. Without fermentation, the taste cannot be guaranteed. A book is a vessel filled with the author's life." Could you share a message of

encouragement with science and technology professionals who aspire to become authors or dream of writing books?

Just as all things mature, so do the words of an author [Image source: Pixabay]

Writing a book isn't limited to experts; rather, I believe that anyone who writes becomes an expert in that field. Writing isn't solely reserved for great people or authors. Anyone can write a book. Don't think you lack material related to writing. Our lives themselves are books. Everyone has their own unique life. Just as the French writer Roland Barthes said, "To make one's life immortal is to write," when we reflect on our own lives, we can say that we've lived precious lives. If you capture these moments in chapters before they volatilize, anyone can become an author.

It's perfectly okay to write essays about what you've experienced and realized in your field, rather than relying solely on expert knowledge. I believe there's a great need for science communicators who can bridge the gap between the general public and scientific and technological fields regardless of the genre. I hope you remember that anyone can write, and I wholeheartedly encourage science and technology professionals who aspire to write.

Source: Korea Institute of Human Resources Development in Science and Technology (KIRD) K-CLUB Interviews

Interview book: Written by Knowledge Ecologist Yoo Yeongman, Namu Saenggak "Writing a Book Requires Great Effort"

BOOKS ARE THE BLOSSOMS OF LOVE

Every human being is a poet. We embroider the art of life in our way, in our language. There is no right or wrong in life. What is most true to oneself is the most beautiful. I am happy to be able to share the gift of books.

One of the gifts books have given me is the joy of writing poetry. It gave me the joy of seeing the beauty of nature and expressing it through letters.

I am writing about the beauty of nature as a poem in ten letters.

Reading takes me to the optimal place where I need to be after a long time has passed. That is the role of the book. The great friends in the book naturally guide you. When we walk steadily without giving up, all things in creation also help us. You have to believe in yourself and keep going until the end. As you move forward, you will encounter a clear sea. You find yourself swimming there.

One of the greatest gifts of reading is gratitude. This gratitude came from the seed of love. When you love, you smell of gratitude and wear the clothes of kindness. Kindness is the lightest clothing in the world. It is a gift like air. Love breeds gratitude and gratitude breeds kindness.

A book is like a magic lamp. If you want wealth, wealth will be given to you. If you want love, it will be given to you. If you want knowledge, knowledge will be given to you. If you want happiness, it will give you happiness. Because you will choose the book you want.

The magic lamp called a book returns exactly what I want. The secret to happiness is in that magic lamp. It is hidden in the typeface created by humans.

The secret to happiness is to touch the heart inside me.
Doing right with my body means doing right with my heart.
Being courteous to your body means being courteous to your heart.

What makes my body happy, makes my heart happy.
The universe of my body is right inside my heart.

We are the owners of the heart.

Fill my body with love and my heart will rejoice.
Fill my body with gratitude and my heart will dance.
The secret to happiness lies in the heart.
That is, it is inside.

Get along well with your inner master.
Laugh well with your inner master.

What is inside is the true me.
It's my universe.
The universe in my mind is a mirror of reality.

If the stream is wide, it flows smoothly. When there is an obstacle and the water narrows, the current becomes faster. Even the sound becomes louder. Then, once it becomes spacious, it flows beautifully. Our mind is also like this. Books are what help us broaden our minds.

You must cherish and love yourself along with books. We must give plenty of loving energy through books. The stronger the energy of love, the more the energy of my happiness is proportional to the speed of light. Let's embrace the light called a book in our hearts. The day will soon come when that light will shine brightly in the most authentic way.

When light finds a small crevice, it illuminates the widest extent of its reach. The more intense the light, the broader the scope. The more intense your inner hopes, the stronger your inner faith, that light becomes more beautiful. The brilliant light you desire is already present within books.

Cherish and love yourself along with books. Through books, share the energy of love abundantly. The stronger the energy of love, the faster your energy of happiness will correspond with the speed of light. Let us embrace the light of books within our hearts. When the time is right, we will shine as brilliantly as the moonlight, true to ourselves.

Seeds of book flowers in my heart,
sown and tended over time,
turn into a garden of blossoms.

Book flowers here.
Book flowers there.
When the fragrance of books fills the air,

our hearts are filled with the songs of birds
And butterflies gather.

When blossoms of light shine throughout the world,
the fragrance of flowers fills the Earth,
the light of blossoms fills the universe.

You and I, inhaling the fragrance of flowers.
Let's journey through a beautiful life together.

Within the universe, we are one.
Come together book flowers.
World of starry flowers.

Within the universe, we are one.
Come together book lights.
Galaxy of Love lights.

The blossom of love,
the blossom of gratitude,
the blossom of happiness,
are book flowers.

How shall we paint the art of life? When book flowers across the globe bloom in harmony, the beautiful Earth adorns itself with laughter. Let's gift books, the magic lamps, to humanity. Let's gift book flowers to the canvas of life. When your book flower and my book flower bloom, a beautiful field of books, a happy world, will come to be. When the light of books shines across the world, our hearts will form rainbows.

Books are the blossoms of hope. The blossoms of love.

To all those who contributed to
bringing forth this book with the light of love,
I express my heartfelt gratitude.

I send my heartfelt blessings,
Ella Yoon